The Integrated Curriculum

The Integrated Curriculum

Books for Reluctant Readers,
Grades 2-5

Anthony D. Fredericks
Assistant Professor of Education
York College
York, Pennsylvania

Illustrated by
Robert Michael Seufert
and
Anthony Allan Stoner

1992
Teacher Ideas Press
A Division of
Libraries Unlimited, Inc.
Englewood, Colorado

To Jesse Moore and Fred Fedorko of East Stroudsburg University — for all the years of friendship, collegiality, and good humor!

TEACHER IDEAS PRESS
A Division of
Libraries Unlimited, Inc.
P.O. Box 6633
Englewood, CO 80155-6633

Library of Congress Cataloging-in-Publication Data

Fredericks, Anthony D.
    The integrated curriculum : books for reluctant readers, grades
2-5 / Anthony D. Fredericks ; illustrated by Robert Michael Seufert
and Anthony Allan Stoner.
    xiv, 187 p. 22x28 cm.
    Includes bibliographical references (p. 173) and index.
    ISBN 0-87287-994-1
    1. Reading (Elementary)--United States--Language experience
approach--Handbooks, manuals, etc. 2. Interdisciplinary approach in
education--United States--Handbooks, manuals, etc. 3. Language
arts--Correlation with content subjects--United States--Handbooks,
manuals, etc. I. Title.
LB1573.33.F74 1992
372.4'1--dc20   92-7546
                                             CIP

CONTENTS

Part 3
MORE SUGGESTED BOOKS FOR RELUCTANT READERS

PREFACE

I guess I have always been a reader. When I got my first flashlight as a kid, I would crawl under the covers at night to read the latest Hardy Boys mystery. (I will never forget my shock when I discovered that there was no author named "Franklin W. Dixon" and that the Hardy Boys were the product of a syndicate of writers.) Later, in prep school, my teachers would complain to my parents that I needed to spend more time with my textbooks and less time with the novels in the school library. Now, as an adult, I am still a voracious reader, reading everything from business books (*Growing a Business*, by Paul Hawken) to science books (*Digging Up Dinosaurs*, by John Horner) to travelogues (*A Life on the Road*, by Charles Kuralt) to books on writing (*Writing to Learn*, by William Zinsser) to humor (*Dave Barry's Greatest Hits*, by Dave Barry) to cartoons (The Far Side Gallery series by Gary Larson).

I am not sure how this insatiable appetite got started, but I suspect that I have always been surrounded by books and was always encouraged to read those books. While I was growing up in southern California, our home was filled with books of every size and shape. My parents were readers, too, subscribers to magazines and book clubs, ardent readers of *The Los Angeles Times*, and sharers of things learned in their readings during dinner-table conversations. As my first role models, they showed me the enjoyment and information that can come from books.

I was fortunate, also, to attend schools where books and literature were prized and valued. St. Matthew's School in Pacific Palisades, California, and the Orme School in Mayer, Arizona, made reading a high priority in every course. Textbooks were frequently supplemented with required readings in the library, courses were enhanced with lists of supplemental books, and reading the classics during the summer months was strongly encouraged. My elementary and high school years were filled with books, literature, and opportunities to share them with classmates and teachers in a variety of ways. (I suspect that my intensely literate background was a major impetus for my decision to become a teacher.)

Before you read more about this book, now is a good time to stop and complete the self-evaluative questionnaire that follows. It is designed to help you assess your commitment to a literature-based reading program for reluctant readers. You may wish to use the results of this informal survey to determine instructional areas or beliefs that may need strengthening. All of the items are prevalent in a fully functioning and dynamic reading program; all of the areas are important in helping reluctant readers achieve a measure of success in reading as well as in other subjects.

I suggest that you fill out this questionnaire at least twice: at the beginning of the year and at the midterm to assess areas needing improvement as well as areas in which you have grown. This self-examination helps you to establish a classroom environment that promotes reading and effectively impacts students' learning and reading potential.

Self-Evaluative Questionnaire

Directions: This questionnaire is designed to provide you with some insights into your efforts to promote reading in the classroom. Place an "S" in front of a statement if it is a strength for you, a "W" if that statement is a weakness for you, and a "U" if you are uncertain. It is hoped that you will have a preponderance of S's on the questionnaire. Areas that you assign a W or U are ones you may need to give some attention to in terms of your efforts to motivate reluctant readers.

_____ 1. Students see me reading from a wide variety of materials, such as magazines, books, newspapers, and the like.

_____ 2. Students have access to many different types of reading materials, including but not limited to books.

_____ 3. I make time during the course of the day when I read to students, even if they are able to read on their own.

_____ 4. I assist students in selecting reading materials in keeping with their interests, desires, and needs.

_____ 5. I make a conscious effort to give students positive reinforcement on their reading progress.

_____ 6. I provide opportunities for students to evaluate and monitor their own progress in reading.

_____ 7. I try not to impose my interests on students' book selections, but rather provide an arena in which students can select their own reading materials.

_____ 8. I relate the world of reading to the world outside my classroom so that students will see those relationships.

_____ 9. I encourage students to share their book experiences with other members of the class.

_____ 10. I promote reading as a natural, normal, and valuable part of everyone's everyday life.

_____ 11. Reading-related activities are *never* used as a disciplinary measure.

_____ 12. My approach to reading is child-centered rather than teacher-centered.

_____ 13. I am aware of the influence of the mass media (television, movies, etc.) and try to promote reading as an important and viable option.

_____ 14. I actively solicit the opinions of students in establishing and promoting the goals and objectives of the reading program.

_____ 15. I am a reader and have made reading a natural and normal part of my lifestyle.

The Integrated Curriculum. 1992. Teacher Ideas Press, a division of Libraries Unlimited, Inc., P.O. Box 6633, Englewood, CO 80155-6633

The Integrated Curriculum grew out of my own experiences as a student—one who was constantly surrounded by books—and my work as a reading specialist in helping youngsters develop aptitudes for and attitudes about successful reading. This book also grew out of conversations with teachers from around the country who are concerned about a growing legion of students in their classrooms who can read but are choosing not to. These reluctant readers have not yet been stimulated by a literate lifestyle and thus decide to pursue other kinds of activities. While it is easy for us to blame this on technology (television and video games), the causes for reading reluctance may be more complicated. Indeed, students' perceptions of reading as a natural and normal part of their lifestyles are influenced by many factors, including (but not limited to) parental attitudes and choices, peer pressure, teachers as role models, individual self-concepts, and cultural and societal perceptions of reading.

However, this book is a celebration of reading as a requisite part of every course, every subject, and every student's life. It is my hope that when you make reading a significant element of every part of your curriculum, it will become a significant part of every student's lifestyle. The intent is to demonstrate the power and beauty that can be found when literature is expanded beyond the covers of a single book into every facet of each subject. In so doing, you will assist youngsters in choosing reading as a viable alternative to more passive forms of entertainment.

The projects and activities offered in these pages rightly belong to my students—the students I had as a teacher, as a reading specialist, and as a college professor. They were developed from many discussions, activities, and interactions over the years. In short, they were generated, proposed, and used by students, not a college professor sitting in an ivory tower. What is most interesting about these ideas is the fact that students wanted to emphasize the *processes* of reading rather than the *products*. Students, particularly those in my Chapter I classes, were more concerned with a hands-on, minds-on approach to learning than they were with filling in the blanks on a never-ending supply of workbook pages and skill sheets. As a result, these suggestions are personalized and individualized investigations of *what could be* instead of the commercialized and usual *what is.*

The thirty-nine books listed within these pages (ten for each grade level, grades 2 through 4, and nine for grade 5) have been selected on the basis of their interest level and application to the needs of reluctant readers. They span a wide range of reading abilities and reading interests. I have tried to provide you and your students with a variety of books (all easily accessible in any school or public library) that promote reading as a universal subject—one that cuts across all disciplines and enhances all subject areas.

This book demonstrates that reading can and should be part of every curricular area—science, math, social studies, music, art, and physical education. Using a single book and expanding into each and every area of the elementary curriculum provides students with the opportunity to use literature as extensions of every facet of the curriculum. Students begin to understand that quality literature is the vehicle for the discovery and new ideas. Reading, books, and literature are not confined solely to a basal reader or a textbook. Students see that literature and the other subject areas work in tandem to open doors of discovery and enjoyment.

You are encouraged to use any book or books according to the needs of your students. The titles listed for a particular grade level are not in any particular order but have been identified as appropriate for students who are reading independently at that grade level. Of course, you do not have to restrict the *third-grade books* only to those students reading at a third-grade level. You are certainly encouraged to have students select books (and their accompanying activities) according to their individual needs and abilities.

You are provided with a wide selection of potential activities for each book. Select those activities that will best serve the needs of your program as well as your students. You may elect to choose activities and have students complete them individually, in small or large groups, or as an entire class. It is important for you and your students to work together in deciding on the appropriate or additional activities for each book. When students have a hand in creating their own self-initiated projects, they are motivated to tackle those projects and to learn from them. Plan to use some of the designated projects prior to reading a selected book, during the reading of the book, as well as after a book has been completed by a student or group of students. In this way you will be helping your students understand that reading is a process of personal involvement and discovery that extends far beyond the covers of a single book.

I sincerely hope that you and your students discover a host of energizing ideas for your reading program within the pages of this book. In truth, this is a saturation approach to the teaching and promotion of reading—an approach that says that when youngsters are surrounded by reading, they will be motivated to choose reading. I wish you well in your quest to help reluctant readers become eager readers!

Acknowledgments

I am indebted to many people whose contributions and support made this book a reality.

JoAnn Miller, the head librarian at the Village Library in Jacobus, Pennsylvania, is the quintessential librarian. She moved heaven and earth (and a few places in between) in helping me gather the sources and resources necessary for this book. She is truly the librarian's librarian and a wonderful person to boot!

An enormous note of appreciation goes to a creative group of teacher education students at York College whose enthusiasm for children's literature for ALL youngsters provided much of the inspiration, ideas, and energy for the development of this book:

Vi Albrecht	Vicki Sirman
Tammy Clark	Diane Borgerding
Sabrina Young	Darlene Hill
Jennifer Stouter	Debby Saxmann
Lisa Marchese	Jane Aiken
Jennifer Brown	Mary Lehman
Traci McAlone	Sheri McBride
Debra Townsend	Cinnamon Flickinger
Jim Hoke	

May their classrooms be filled with loads of literature and lots of lifelong readers!

Rob Seufert and Tony Stoner, two friends of my son Jonathan, deserve extra credit for taking time out from a summer of fun and jobs to create the fantastic illustrations for this book. The art world will truly be enhanced by their talent and skill.

All my former students at Sheckler Elementary School in Catasauqua, Pennsylvania, are as much a part of this book as anyone. Their ideas and thoughts about the excitement of reading are liberally sprinkled throughout these pages. I hope you discover their spirit in each and every activity.

My colleagues—Brian, Bonnie, Mary Louise, and Dean—in the education department at York College deserve special recognition for their patience and understanding in dealing with the strange work habits (and equally strange behavior) of their colleague.

As always, this book would not have been possible were it not for the support and constant enthusiasm of my editor, Suzanne Barchers. She is a joy to work with and a marvelous friend besides.

It is my wife Phyllis, however, who deservedly receives the highest commendation of all, the "Fredericks' Medal of Honor." This is given in recognition of having endured a summer of dinners by the light of the computer screen, a (hypothetical) vacation at the shore, and a basement that just never got cleaned out (I promise it will be done by spring!). This book would not have been possible without her constant love and support.

Part 1
Motivating, Connecting, and Comprehending

GOLD STARS, SMELLY STICKERS, AND MOTIVATION

■ _____ ■

When I was in the sixth grade, my teacher, Mrs. MacDonald, had an oversized chart posted in the front left corner of the classroom. The chart listed every student's name down the left-hand side. Next to each name Mrs. MacDonald would place a colored star depending on how one did on the weekly spelling test. The object, I suppose, was to publicly recognize those who had mastered the spelling words for the week as well as to act as an incentive for those who were less than adequate spellers (encouraging them on to spelling *victory*, I guess).

To be perfectly honest with you, I have never been, nor will ever be, the world's greatest speller. In fact, I believe that one of the world's greatest technological advances in the last fifty years (ranking far ahead of manned lunar landings and microwave ovens) is the spell checker on my word-processing program. That single feature has done more to advance my writing career and eliminate my concerns over "i before e, except after c" and other spelling peccadillos than any other discovery or invention of the twentieth century. It is my saving grace and my professional life preserver (already it has located and corrected four spelling errors in the preceding two paragraphs).

Nevertheless, in sixth grade my spelling was in considerably worse shape than it is now. While everyone else was accumulating stars of every size, shape, and color, I lagged far behind my classmates (imagine my distress on parent/teacher night when my lack of spelling prowess went on public display). My best friend, Bill Calendar, was the spelling wizard of sixth grade and was accorded the honor of having two horizontal rows assigned to his name simply because of the sheer number of gold stars he earned over the course of the year. (By the way, Bill is now a vice president with Merrill Lynch. I wonder if there is some sort of correlation between sixth-grade spelling ability and occupational roles?) Yet, by the time June rolled around, there I was stuck in the middle of the chart with only three blue stars next to my name!

Even today, I can still picture that chart in my mind—still plastered to the upper left-hand corner of the sixth-grade classroom—and can still remember how I felt about that public affirmation of my spelling deficits. I am also aware of the fact that the chart did not in any way encourage, stimulate, or motivate me to become a better speller. Rather, it may have been more of a hindrance to my spelling development than Mrs. MacDonald would have ever thought possible.

Now, with more than twenty years of teaching experience under my belt (fifteen of which took place in public and private schools), I have come to the conclusion that motivation, to be effective, must be stimulated but not controlled by the teacher. In other words, as teachers, we must provide opportunities for our students to develop their own internal sense of motivation instead of manipulating them through external means. Awarding gold stars and smelly stickers fosters a competitive approach to learning, against the advice and experience of a growing legion of educators who believe that competitive goal structures heighten student anxiety and avoidance reactions, promote group fragmentation and hostility, and subvert the development of an intrinsic motivation for learning.

Simply stated, motivation comes in two forms. Extrinsic, or external, motivation means that one person has control over another person or that an individual relies on others to establish personal goals and the reward system for those goals. Intrinsic, or internal, motivation, on the other hand, means that individuals make their own decisions and create the power to pursue them, that drive and ambition are determined internally. Common logic supports the notion that intrinsically motivated students do better academically than do extrinsically motivated students. This is due to one or more of the following factors:

1. Extrinsically motivated students are engaged in a competitive atmosphere that becomes self-defeating in the long run.

2. "External" students learn to work only for the rewards at the end; the processes used to achieve those rewards are unimportant.

3. Extrinsic students' emphasis is away from learning. The queries "What grade did I get?" and "How did I do?" are typical indicators of extrinsic students.

4. The students' motivation to learn is subverted to the goal of reward accumulation.

5. External students avoid creativity and problem-solving activities in favor of low-level thinking activities.

6. Students' goals, if any, are short-term and immediate; they avoid long-range projects and thinking.

7. Extrinsic students do not take personal responsibility for their learning, but rather see the things that happen to them as a matter of luck or chance.

8. Extrinsic learners do not see a relationship between effort and achievement.

9. Externalizing becomes a self-perpetuating cycle in which continual lack of academic success substantiates a belief that one may never be successful.

Because there is a strong relationship between motivation and academic achievement, we need to be mindful that the behaviors we exercise in the classroom will lead to heightened levels of motivation and, in turn, heightened levels of achievement. This becomes even more critical when we work with reluctant readers. Since many teachers promote reading as the "universal subject" (as does society in general), students, from very early in their educational careers, learn that reading competence is a strong determinant of academic competence in general. Thus, lack of success or a reluctance to engage in literacy activities is frequently perceived as a serious impediment to total scholastic growth.

Many educators believe that students do not become reluctant readers because of low intelligence, socioeconomic conditions, or lack of materials. Instead, students' reluctance to read is due to the instruction or lack of instruction they receive in the classroom (Allington 1983). That contention is supported by Durkin's study (1978-1979), which found that less than 1 percent of classroom reading time is devoted to comprehension *instruction*. May (1990) discovered that an average child will complete nearly 1,000 workbook pages in reading alone each school year (time in which no instruction takes place). While those statistics may seem pessimistic, they may also support the notion that readers are made, not born.

I support the idea that the teacher is the pre-eminent force (along with parents) in a child's approach to and progress in reading. This belief goes far beyond the instruction any single child receives to include affective factors as well. It also means that the way we approach reading in the classroom has a lot to do with how much children embrace reading as a natural and normal part of their everyday lives. In my own classrooms, I found that too many children regard reading as a school-related or classroom-only activity. These students think of reading as something that takes place only between 9:00 and 10:00 every morning or believe that reading exists solely between the pages of a basal text. As a result, too many youngsters get the idea that reading is regulated by the clock or by some obscure publisher in a distant city. Thus, too many students have a jaundiced view of their literacy growth as something directed by forces out of their control or purview.

My own philosophy of teaching is driven by the idea that teachers act as facilitators of the learning process rather than monitors. By this I mean that when youngsters are given honest and sincere opportunities to select and direct their own learning (and are taught to do just that), they can achieve a measure of independence and motivation that will carry them beyond the four walls of the classroom. In short, what we do in the classroom may be just as important, if not more so, than what we teach. Indeed, I believe the chief role of a competent educator is to guide students to their own discoveries. This means providing them with the tools they need and the necessary instruction to use those tools and then giving them the chance to explore, discover, and investigate the joys and excitement of learning as a personal goal rather than a dictated one.

While that may be easy to say from my perspective as a college professor, it also comes from eleven years of working as a Chapter I reading specialist. It comes from many instructional successes with children as well as a few instructional failures. It comes from conversations with students, parents, and fellow teachers who were looking for creative approaches to reading instruction. Finally, it comes from some gut-level feelings about how I learn, how I hope my college students will learn, and how I hope this next generation of students will embrace learning.

Points to Ponder

If you have taught for any length of time, you have undoubtedly dealt with reluctant readers in your classroom. You have experienced the frustration of working with youngsters in the "low group," trying to provide them with instruction keyed to their needs while juggling the reading demands of other students in the classroom. Or perhaps you are a Chapter I teacher who is seeking to instill a love of reading in all your students and are constantly looking for materials that will help you. No matter what your viewpoint, you are certainly aware that encouraging reluctant readers is an immense challenge, albeit an exciting one.

Here are several procedures and processes gleaned from my own classroom experiences, my work as a Chapter I reading specialist, some current research, conversations with colleagues around the country, and discussions with students themselves. You may wish to consider these for use in motivating the reluctant readers in your classroom. When used in conjunction with the other suggestions in this book, it is hoped that they will enable you to "energize" all the readers under your tutelage.

Give students choices. If you are a typical elementary teacher, you make approximately 1,500 educational decisions every day. You have to decide everything from who collects the lunch money for the day to when to reschedule the language arts lesson because of the special assembly. Although many of your decisions will be small, they must be made nonetheless. I might even go so far as to postulate that a major cause of teacher burnout is the fact that teachers make too many decisions in the classroom, decisions that should and can rightly belong to students (when they have been trained to do so).

Unfortunately, students have very few opportunities to make their own decisions, even when those decisions affect their enjoyment, performance, or mastery of a particular skill or lesson. My experience has shown me that students who are provided with opportunities to make choices become more self-assured and competent. When students feel some control over their reading destinies, they will want to invest more of themselves in those destinies.

Here are some suggestions on how to give students opportunities to make their own choices in a reading program:

- Allow students to select the books they want to read. Do not make all their choices for them.

- Permit reluctant readers to choose specific times to spend in silent reading. Allow students to select their own reading materials and interact with those materials in pleasurable and productive ways. A plethora of paperback books, an abundant and rich classroom library, and access to the school library can all be sources of extra silent-reading materials.

- Allow readers to use books and reading materials in keeping with their abilities and needs. Provide reluctant readers with easy-to-read books to help them achieve a level of fluency and continuity that may not be available in designated grade-level books.

- Help reluctant readers achieve some independence by offering opportunities for them to make decisions and take responsibility for their own individual reading progress. Encourage them to ask their own questions, integrate their background knowledge and experiences, select their own books, design their own activities, and establish their own goals and objectives. By so doing, you help students become less teacher dependent and more independent.

- Focus more on creative, open-ended, and divergent activities that allow for personal interpretations and nonjudgmental evaluations.

- Provide opportunities for students to contribute ideas, plans, expectations, projects, suggestions, techniques, and learning possibilities. Do not rely solely on teacher's manuals or commercial materials.

Involve students in goal setting. Responsible reading occurs when students have opportunities to establish individual goals, monitor those goals, assess those goals, and make decisions on how they can become more actively involved in the reading process. Competent readers do this quite naturally, often without thinking. That may be because they have assumed a measure of independence in reading or because they are more internally motivated than the reluctant or remedial readers in a classroom.

Reluctant readers are known by many labels, but it is important to note that their drive or level of motivation often depends on what others say or how others react to their reading performance. In short, reluctant readers have a tendency to be teacher-dependent rather than independent. Helping students achieve a level of independence and self-assurance leads to higher levels of motivation and more positive self-concept.

Table 1, "Things to Ask Myself When I Read," (see page 21) provides a series of monitoring questions students can ask themselves as they read. Obviously, you do not want students to ask all these questions every time they read. Instead, your intent is to have students begin to internalize some of these questions at each of the three major stages of reading. In so doing, they are taking a major step forward in becoming more responsible and more motivated readers.

Allow students self-assessment opportunities. One very productive method teachers can use to help students assume a measure of responsibility is to have them engage in some self-assessment procedures. With self-assessment, students can begin to take control over their individual reading destinies and become more independent readers. When independence is fostered, reluctance to read is diminished. The result is students who read because they have a personal stake in what is read.

You can use the following procedures to help students engage in a process of self-assessment. Many of these strategies can be implemented in a wide variety of classroom activities and can be used for specific individuals as well as small and large groups. I suggest that you consider using one or more of these frequently.

- Provide opportunities for students to establish their own goals for reading a selection. Afterward, encourage them to decide if those goals were attained.

- Have students design one-third of the questions for any tests or quizzes.

- Design a formal evaluation instrument on a story or book. Instead of having students respond with answers to the questions, ask them to indicate (for each question) whether they 1) positively know the answer, 2) are mostly sure of the answer, 3) have some idea of the answer, or 4) have no idea what the answer is. Discuss and share reasons (via individual conferences) why students responded as they did.

- Ask students to evaluate the questions in the teacher's edition of the basal text. Encourage them to design a system that rates the queries in terms of difficulty, appropriateness, level of cognition, or any other criterion.

- Encourage students to explain their reasons for selecting answers to specific questions.

- Stimulate the development of student-generated questions instead of relying on textual questions.

- Model your own metacognitive processes as you read aloud to students (see pages 33-35).

- Provide opportunities for students to explain why they understood or did not understand parts of a reading selection.

- Stimulate students to think beyond single right answers.

- Allow students to frequently evaluate their own predictions, purposes, and questions. The intent is not to validate "right answers," but rather to illustrate reading as an active and constructive process.

- Suspend judgment when asking questions and redirect queries to get multiple responses.

- Allow students to state their own expectations or criteria for assignments.

- Provide opportunities for students to compile lists of things they learned from a lesson as well as things they did not understand. Take time to discuss those lists.

- Permit students to rate any one of your lessons in terms of *their* level of comprehension. In other words, did your presentation promote understanding and interest? Discuss your reactions in terms of their perceptions.

- Encourage students to reflect on their errors and what they can learn from them.

- Help students assume responsibility for their own learning through activities in which they set, monitor, and assess their own personal goals.

- Provide a variety of self-correcting assignments within each unit of study.

Provide lots of recreational reading. Have poor readers spend lots of time in recreational reading. Provide opportunities for them to share and discuss what they read, not to measure their reading progress but to offer insights into the nature of reading as a communicative act.

Promote a whole classroom approach to reading. Build a community of readers. Do not isolate reluctant readers with labels such as "Bluebirds," "Ninja Turtles," or "Iguanas." In short, reduce ability grouping. An important body of research (including John Goodlad's classic *A Place Called School* [1984]) demonstrates that in low-ability groups less time is spent on each task, less learning occurs, and the quality of teaching is less than in heterogeneous groups. In other words, provide sufficient opportunities for readers of all levels and ability to interact with one another. Engage all students in processes and activities that allow them to interpret, discuss, and process, in engaging and interactive ways, information learned from reading.

Make reading cross-curricular. Integrate reading into all areas of the curriculum. Try to break away from the idea that reading occurs only during a specific time of the day or within specific kinds of books, such as textbooks. Design and develop activities through which reading and literature become an inherent and intrinsic part of each curricular area. Make reading instruction part of the instruction in every subject. In essence, you want to design a broad-based reading program that includes all the language arts in all the content areas. Demonstrate the relationships reading has to speaking, writing, and listening and promote those relationships throughout every facet of children's literacy growth.

Design a community of readers. Provide students with numerous opportunities to share their reading with each other. Many students have the mistaken impression that reading is something that takes place solely between one author and one reader. Emphasizing a community of readers/sharers can have enormous benefits for the reluctant reader, not the least of which is a support system that encourages reading discoveries.

You can foster a cooperative spirit in your classroom by encouraging *all* students, irrespective of academic ability, to engage in participatory activities together. Mixed-ability groups allow every student to demonstrate competence and to feel a sense of belonging, usefulness, and personal potency. Most significantly, the research shows that in cooperative learning classrooms academic and affective performance improves for both advantaged *and* disadvantaged learners (Sagor 1988).

Build strong ties to school and public libraries. Librarians have much to contribute to both teachers and students. Work with them to create a revolving classroom collection, foster reading activities, arrange author visits and book talks, assemble good book lists, manage book discussions and state reading award programs, provide one-to-one reading guidance, and provide a host of other services. Librarians can supply teachers with the best read-alouds and the latest and best of each new crop of books.

Make reading literature-based. A literature-based reading program has numerous advantages that set it apart from traditional basal-based or skill-based programs. It promotes reading for meaning, reading for pleasure, and reading for personal development. Flooding your classroom with loads of good books can stimulate the development of positive attitudes as well as positive cognitive growth.

Model appropriate reading behaviors. Be an enthusiastic role model for students. Embrace reading as a natural and normal part of your lifestyle. Be excited about the reading activities you promote in the classroom. Share your reading experiences with students. Model the reading behaviors you would like your students to emulate. If you are "energized" about reading, your students will be, too. In other words, be a student yourself.

Create a positive environment. Create an atmosphere of high expectation in your classroom. Let underachievers know that you expect high levels of performance from them and will not tolerate shoddy or less than adequate work. In other words, make sure your reluctant readers are given the same academic opportunities as are the motivated readers. Are they given equal amounts of time for responding to questions, completing assignments, and participating in all reading-related activities?

Meet students' needs. Be aware of the learning styles exhibited by the students in your classroom. Many teachers have discovered that reluctant readers tend to prefer a hands-on, practical approach to learning. They are frustrated when involved in abstract activities (writing essays, determining sequence) and motivated when involved in experiential activities (creating a model, designing a collage).

Personal Reflections

During my four years as a classroom teacher and eleven years as a Chapter I teacher, my students taught me many things. Here are three important lessons I have learned from more than a decade of work with reluctant readers.

Students do not have to read every book. One of the great joys of a literature-rich classroom is that there are many books for every reading taste, interest, and inclination. However, this does not mean that every student needs to read every book—what it means is that there is something for everyone. My own Chapter I classroom had nearly 2,500 paperback books organized into three dozen or more categories (sports, mysteries, space exploration, dinosaurs, etc.). By using a series of interest inventories (see table 2, page 22) I was able to direct students to those books that best met their needs and interests. It was not necessary or important for them to read every book in the room, but it was vitally important for them to have access to a variety of books.

Students do not have to like every book. As adults, we often read books because they were recommended to us, we saw a favorable review in a magazine or journal, or we were familiar with the author. But that does not guarantee that we will or should like the new book. Children should have that same decision-making power, too. Too often, children are forced to read books because those books have been designated as "appropriate" for their age or ability, but that designation does not imply that a particular book will or should be enjoyed. In fact, it is most appropriate to establish a student rating system by which students rate the interest level(s) of the books they read (see table 3, page 24.) This can be a powerful motivator, because students will often read a book (or choose not to read a book) simply because another student gave it a high (or low) rating. I had students do this in my classroom by placing a small self-stick dot (available in any stationery or office supply store) on the back of any books they read. We used a series of five color-coded dots (red = highly recommended, green = recommended, blue = OK, yellow = bad choice, orange = really rotten). Students could then check the back of each book to see what their fellow students thought of the book and make a decision on whether they wanted to read it.

Students do not have to finish every book. Very few adults finish every book they begin. There is certainly no reason for students to have to complete every single book they pick up either. In fact, if children feel that, after a couple of pages, a selected book just will not hold their interest, they should have the choice of putting the book back and selecting another one. Such choices give students more opportunities to make their own decisions and become more independent readers. That alone can be a powerful motivating force in any program designed for reluctant readers.

What should be evident from these statements is the fact that students who are given choices within a reading program are likely to assume a sense of responsibility within that program. In other words, independence is fostered and reading growth is maximized when self-initiated responsibility drives students' ventures into the wide and wonderful world of reading and literature.

I've come to a frightening conclusion that I am the decisive element in the classroom. It's my personal approach that creates the climate. It's my daily mood that makes the weather. As a teacher, I have a tremendous power to make a child's life miserable or joyous. I can be a tool of torture or an instrument of inspiration. I can humiliate or humor, hurt or heal. In all situations, it is my response that decides whether a crisis will be escalated or deescalated and a child humanized or dehumanized. (Hiam G. Ginott 1972)

Reference List

Allington, Richard. 1983. "The Reading Instruction Provided Readers of Differing Abilities." *Elementary School Journal* 83, no. 5: 548-59.

Durkin, Delores. 1978-1979. "What Classroom Observations Reveal about Reading Comprehension Instruction." *Reading Research Quarterly* 14, no. 4: 481-533.

May, Frank B. 1990. *Reading as Communication.* Columbus, OH: Merrill.

Ginott, Hiam G. 1972. *Teacher and Child: A Book for Parents and Teachers.* New York: Macmillan.

Goodlad, John. 1984. *A Place Called School.* New York: McGraw-Hill.

Sagor, Richard. 1988. "Teetering ... On the Edge of Failure." *Learning '88* 17, no. 8 (April): 28-34.

WHOLE LANGUAGE AND RELUCTANT READERS

In the early 1970s I was a member of the U.S. Coast Guard and was stationed at the Recruit Training Center in Alameda, California. The Coast Guard maintained two recruit training centers (the other being in Cape May, New Jersey). At that time, during the height of the Vietnam War, it was becoming apparent to the Coast Guard that significant numbers of recruits were entering the service with only a modicum of academic skills. Even though the Coast Guard required a high-school diploma as part of its entrance requirements, it seemed as though large numbers of young people were entering with the third- and fourth-grade reading levels. As the academic requirements of boot camp necessitated an approximate reading level of ninth grade, many recruits had to be discharged from the Coast Guard for inadequate academic skills.

At that particular time, I was working in the Personnel Office and noticed the large amount of correspondence that was being sent back and forth from both training centers and Coast Guard headquarters in Washington, DC. Having an education background, I decided to draft a proposal for a remedial program that would provide academically deficient recruits with the reading skills they needed. My plan was to take a block of four weeks (inserted in the middle of the eight-week training program) and provide these young people with seven hours of instruction, five days a week, for the four-week period. The Coast Guard liked the proposal and quickly moved to establish the program, which was the only one of its kind in the Coast Guard (although the Navy and the Army had had programs for academically deficient recruits for some time).

What made the program intriguing, as I began to put it together, was that the Coast Guard gave me *carte blanche* for the final design and materials. In other words, I could spend any amount of money I wanted to obtain needed materials and equipment. Well, with a mandate like that I was tempted to get lots of everything. For weeks I pored over catalogs, visited high schools with similar programs, talked with experts, and visited exemplary program sites throughout California.

Although money was no object, I soon realized that the most successful and effective programs relied not on fancy machines, loads of training manuals, or heaps of skill sheets, but on the utilization of a variety of reading materials—namely, paperback books. Thus, I filled my classroom with tables and bookcases full of paperbacks ordered from a small number of catalogs. The program that evolved was based not on mastering the Coast Guard training manuals but on enjoying and sharing good literature. My students and I talked about books, shared any number of extending activities about books, related books to our lives and background experiences, and surrounded ourselves with all manner of literature. What I did not know at that time was that we were immersed in a whole language approach to the successful completion of boot camp. (Incidentally, the program achieved a success rate of 84 percent—that is, 84 percent of the recruits who would have been sent home for academic deficiencies were able to successfully complete the scholastic requirements of recruit training and become full-fledged coast guard members.)

Years later, when I became a Chapter I reading specialist and had my own classroom, I took the same tack. I filled my classroom with loads and loads of books. Each year when I was assigned my annual budget (unfortunately, I never had *carte blanche* again), I ordered enough paperback books to flood the room with them. I had books cascading down from the ceiling, bookcases overflowing in every corner of the room, shelves piled high with both fiction and nonfiction, and reading tables loaded with even more books. The room became a second library of sorts (it was not unusual for non-Chapter I students to stop by the room on their way to their classrooms in the morning to check out a book or two). My students and I reveled in books and literature of all kinds and all dimensions, engaging in activities that promoted reading, writing, listening, and speaking in a host of meaningful contexts. By the time I left the public school, that classroom had nearly 2,500 paperback books—and not one single workbook. Once again, that remedial program proved to be fantastically successful. Students were checking out more books from the library, cooperative activities flourished, excitement ran high, and motivation for reading was intense.

Although much of my support for literature-based reading programs comes from my own first-hand experiences, I have since discovered that there is an abundance of research that also supports this approach to reading instruction. Cooper (1990) provides an exhaustive review of over seventeen research studies, all of which indicate that students in literature-rich classrooms demonstrate above-average comprehension as well as strong reading skills. That evidence applies equally to average students and to students experiencing some reading difficulties. If the two major programs

I have been associated with are any indication, students (secondary and elementary) can reap enormous literacy benefits when they are surrounded by literature and provided with activities that have intrinsic meaning for them.

What I am suggesting is that reluctant readers can benefit as much or more from a whole language approach to reading instruction as the so-called "on level" students can. As Cooper (1990) emphasized, isolated skill work actually runs counter to the way children learn and use language. Language is processed holistically and thus must be presented in an instructional setting in a similar fashion. A whole language approach to learning has magnificent possibilities for readers who are less than enthusiastic about reading or deficient in specific reading skills.

Whole Language Approach

I define *whole language* as the integration of reading, writing, speaking, and listening into a context that is meaningful to the child. Whole language offers students a framework for learning in which self-initiated goals are established, literature abounds, skills are taught in a meaningful context, and purposeful activities are interwoven into all dimensions of the curriculum. Thus, whole language is not a program but a philosophy of teaching and learning that is child centered and contextually based (Fredericks 1991).

The whole language philosophy of teaching is also based on the successful integration of children's literature throughout the curriculum. Literature provides the vehicle by which children can travel to all parts of the elementary curriculum, observing and appreciating the scenery along the way. In short, children are given choices (as is the teacher) to actively participate according to abilities and interests. Obviously, this means relinquishing some typical teacher responsibilities and transferring some of those responsibilities to the children, giving them more freedom to process learning rather than just memorize facts. In the long run, whole language helps children develop their creative and critical thinking abilities in a meaningful and relevant context. Filling in worksheets from a commercial publisher does not necessarily develop critical thinking; deciding on the format for a skit pertinent to a particular piece of literature does (Fredericks 1991).

A whole language approach to reading fosters the creation of personal responses to learning, particularly when children are provided with opportunities to engage in purposeful activities that evolve from a literature-rich environment. Using both objective and subjective evidence, Shumaker and Shumaker (1988) present a convincing argument for a whole language, whole literature design for reluctant readers. They argue that a literature-based reading program has the following benefits for reluctant readers:

1. It revitalizes and enriches the experiences of reluctant readers.

2. It provides such students with new frames of reference for reading, frames that are not evident in skill-based programs.

3. It has a significant and positive impact on the performance and attitudes of reluctant readers.

4. It introduces great authors to readers who might not otherwise encounter them.

5. It enhances the writing ability of students by exposing them to the holistic writing of others.

6. It can supply a potent form of bibliotherapy.

7. It enhances the child's self-concept and reduces the isolation of the struggling student.

8. It offers high interest, excellent models, real language use, and a rich linguistic environment from which to abstract language skills.

The Shumakers convincingly demonstrate that children's literature should be at the center of any reading program, particularly one for reluctant readers. To that argument I would add that children's literature forms the foundation of a successful literacy program—a foundation from which whole language activities can emanate. Given the previous definition, it seems that a whole language approach to the challenge of reluctant readers holds tremendous promise and possibility in helping all youngsters achieve a measure of reading success and appreciation.

Connecting with Literature

Take a few moments and think about the following quotations:

> Literature must be at the center of the reading program; otherwise, reading is merely a collection of learned skills. Reading skills are of little worth if students do not have the desire to read. Literature can motivate children and instill in them a lifelong desire to read. (Stoodt 1989)

> If we teach a child to read, yet develop not the taste for reading all our teaching is for naught. We shall have produced a nation of "illiterate literates"—those who know how to read, but do not read. (Huck 1979)

What should be evident from such statements is that authorities in the field of reading instruction realize and recognize the value of a literature-based reading program. What is even more significant is the idea that a literature-rich classroom can provide reluctant readers with the incentive and opportunity to become active participants in their own literacy growth.

According to Huus (1975), literature is used in classrooms in five general ways:

1. Free reading, which occurs during the time set aside for students to read books that they choose on their own.

2. Reading aloud to children. Children should be prepared for these readings and selections should be carefully chosen.

3. A guided and supplementary reading program in which students receive assistance in selecting books.

4. Topical units of study, which may focus on such topics as "Christmas in Other Lands," or "Arbor Day." During this unit, students read fiction, nonfiction, and poetry that are related to the selected unit.

5. *Creative sharing of literature* (emphasis mine). The total literature program incorporates all of the preceding approaches in a flexible instructional plan. This type of program encourages students to appreciate literature.

It should be evident that literature has tremendous possibilities for re-encouraging and re-energizing reluctant readers. When youngsters are immersed in a literature-rich reading program, their creative thinking and problem-solving abilities are stimulated, their affective development is enhanced, bonds between their prior knowledge and textual knowledge are cemented, and literacy learning becomes an ever-expanding process of discovery and exploration.

The Integrated Curriculum: Books for Reluctant Readers, Grades 2-5 provides literature-based, whole language activities designed to open up learning possibilities for the reluctant readers in your classroom. These activities have been designed to enrich and expand your reading program by: 1) encouraging students' divergent thinking processes; 2) allowing students to interact in social and mutually beneficial relationships; 3) stimulating students' independence in learning, problem solving, and reading; and 4) promoting students' creativity and originality throughout their literacy growth.

You should feel free to select, adapt, or modify activities in keeping with the needs and abilities of your students. Also, be sure to provide students with many chances to select activities and learning opportunities that have meaning for them. In so doing, you will be providing them with a personal stake in their individual literacy development. Obviously, no single activity is appropriate for every student in your room, nor should all students attempt to complete identical activities. Since there are many interpretations of literature, children should be allowed to pursue and elaborate on activities that will enhance their appreciation of the material read and emphasize the significance of literature as a vehicle for learning.

Beyond Book Reports

To be honest with you I do not like book reports (at least, the traditional ones). I hated them as a kid, I despised them as a teacher, and I abhor them now. The reasons for my displeasure with book reports are many. First, unless students are going to grow up to become book critics, the requirements of listing author, publisher, copyright date, summary, and the like seldom does any good. It is a series of mechanical acts that remains the same every time and holds little interest or fascination for the students doing it. I equate it with students writing "I will not throw spitballs" 500 times on the chalkboard. It is certain that they will probably never throw spitballs again (or at least not get caught doing it next time), but it is equally certain that they will hate writing as a result of that obnoxious assignment.

Second, traditional book reports are done for the convenience of the teacher. They are assigned by the teacher and completed according to the teacher's directions. Students rarely have an opportunity to be creative and inventive in the traditional book-report format. The setup is so universal and standard that imagination is severely hampered and elaboration is seldom encouraged. What results is a series of "cookie-cutter" book reports that sound and look the same, even though they are easier to grade.

Third, a book report is just what its name implies: a report on a book. It is perceived by most students as a way for teachers to check if the student really read the book (although many book reports have been written with only a cursory glance at the book itself). Students quickly get a sense that the object is to determine whether the book was read, not to see if it was enjoyed. In short, getting students to read required books rather than to enjoy a variety of literature seems to be the primary objective of the book-reporting process.

Fourth, and perhaps most important, is the fact that the application of a book to students' lives is not promoted by a traditional book report and may not even be discussed. Rarely do youngsters preparing book reports have opportunities to extend the book into their own lives or understand the relationships between books within a similar genre or topic. The role of literature as an important element in children's lives needs to be at the very center of any classroom reading program. Generating an endless stream of book reports does little to promote that concept and may actually be a detriment to children's appreciation and enjoyment of quality literature.

What I suggest instead is a variety of extending activities that provide youngsters with opportunities to become actively involved in the dynamics of individual books, empathizing with the characters, visualizing the settings, comprehending the plots and themes, and creatively experiencing the intentions of the author. It is critical to remember that an effective reading program is based on the opportunities children have to make an investment of self. By that I mean that students are provided with an arena that allows them to make choices and carry out those choices, so that reading becomes more personal and enjoyable. Telling students that they must read a certain book and write a particular kind of book report may actually hamper children's enjoyment and growth in reading. On the other hand, when we give children the chance to engage in a process of self-selection, we tell them that they can become active decision makers and *processors* of their own literacy growth.

Included here is a long list of book extensions that could be part of your reading program. These extensions will be most effective when children are given the chance to select the ones that meet their individual needs and interests. In short, they should not be *assigned*, but rather should be *offered*. If you do so, you will help students develop a measure of independence and autonomy within the reading program and eventually within all areas of your classroom curriculum.

Please feel free to alter or modify any of these suggestions in keeping with the dynamics of your own classroom and the individual strengths of students in that classroom. Allow children opportunities to alter or elaborate any activity according to their designs or creative responses. These suggestions are directed to the students. You may wish to collect these book extensions in a notebook or post them on a wall of the classroom for all students to review periodically. You may read selections out loud to younger students.

Book Extensions

Auction. Bring in old paperback books, of various types, that have been stored at home. Work with other students to scour your neighborhoods to locate other books. Hold a book auction during a lunch period or at the end of the school day. Donate the proceeds to the local library for the purchase of new children's books.

Book of the Month. Work with other students to establish some book clubs in the school. These book clubs can meet either before or after school to discuss new books, make book recommendations to parents for gifts, or even make recommendations to the school librarian for specific purchases.

Buddy-Buddy. Set up peer reading groups around the school. Pair up with students from different rooms to read together or to share ideas about specific books or authors. These mini-groups could be combined periodically for large-group discussions throughout the year.

Coming Attractions. At the beginning of each month, make up a colorful poster that advertises a specific reading topic, new book release, or collection of books by a favorite author. Posters on "Sports Stories" or "Books by Laura Ingalls Wilder" can be placed in either the classroom or school for display.

Author(ities). Work together in small groups to write, illustrate, and produce your own books. Stories in these books can be language experience stories or other types of creative writing. Plan to set up a special display of these books in the school library. Donate some of the books to the local library.

People in the Street. Interview people concerning their reading interests or preferences. Collect information on their occupations, interests and hobbies, or recollections of popular books and materials that were used when they were in school. What people remember most about their own reading experiences in school is a possible project also.

Puppet Theater. Design and produce a puppet show based on a book. Schedule this show for visits to other rooms in the school or in lower grades. Videotape them for presentation at a lunch hour or in individual classrooms.

Role Play. Create a simple play based on characters or scenes in a favorite book or story. Make arrangements with the local public library to put on your play for younger readers. Consider presenting productions at a children's hospital or day-care center.

Cover Up. Select several favorite books from the school library and create new dust covers. Make arrangements with the school librarian to create a special display area where these books and your newly designed jackets can be shown off.

Picture This. Set up special bulletin boards around the school or within the local community to advertise favorite books. Focus on the most exciting, scariest, or saddest parts of a book to get others to read it. Change displays frequently to provide variety and excitement.

Ad Agency. Develop several magazine-type advertisements for favorite books. Collect these advertisements into a portfolio for distribution within the school or district. Create several large, advertisement-type posters and submit them to the local library for display.

Movie Review. Obtain several cardboard shoeboxes and cut out rectangles in the short side of each one. Create hand-rolled "movies" on adding-machine tape to be rolled through each cut-out section of a box, using pencils or dowels as rollers. These movies can include scenes from favorite books and should be sent to other classrooms.

Party Time. Make arrangements for an all-school, or all-grade-level costume party to which everyone comes dressed as their favorite storybook character (teachers too!). Invite a local book author, schedule book readings, or present dramatizations of popular stories. Award prizes for characterizations most in keeping with the themes of the respective books.

The Integrated Curriculum. 1992. Teacher Ideas Press, a division of Libraries Unlimited, Inc., P.O. Box 6633, Englewood, CO 80155-6633

Additional Book Extension Projects

- Select a "reading buddy" and set aside a certain time during the day when the two of you can read to each other.

- Practice reading a primary-level book and then read it aloud to a kindergarten class.

- Make a poster that advertises a specific reading topic of the month such as "Sports Stories" or "Mysteries."

- Tape record a portion of a book so other students can enjoy it.

- Invite your mother, father, or grandparents to read a book so you can discuss it together.

- Illustrate the most exciting, scariest, saddest, or happiest part of the book.

- Draw an imaginary setting for the book. What types of illustrations would you include in the book that are not there now?

- Make a crossword puzzle using the names, places, and events from the book.

- Write a series of questions that can be attached to the book for others to answer.

- Make a collage of important events in the book. Cut out pictures from old magazines and paste them on a sheet of construction paper.

- Work with some friends in writing a song for the book. Take the tune from one of your favorite songs and rewrite the words using words from the book.

- With all your classmates, vote for the favorite book of the month.

- Invent a comic strip using the characters and events in the book.

- Write a letter of appreciation to the author of the book telling him or her why you enjoyed it.

- Evaluate several books in the class library. Work with your classmates in setting up some sort of rating system (1 to 5; high to low, excellent to poor) to gauge each book.

- Read a new book (or part of a book) each day.

- Write a letter to a friend about what you are learning from the book.

- Read several different books on the same topic.

- Read several books by the same author.

- Keep a journal or diary on your impressions of the book as you read it.

- Make up a newspaper about the book or the events in it.

- Create a fictional journal about a figure in the book.

- Write an original adaptation of an event from a book.

- Set up a "Reading Corner" filled with periodicals, books, and other printed materials concerning the subject of the book.

- Collect or create recipes the book characters might enjoy and write a cookbook.

- Design a wordless picture-book edition of the story.

- Create an original adaptation or retelling of the book's story.

- Share the book with a classmate or partner.

- Write a newspaper article on an important event from the book.

- Locate and read a relevant magazine article about something that happens in the book.

- With some friends, write an original play.

- Write a poem about something in the book.

- Write a letter to a character or historical figure.

- Write a sequel or prequel to an incident or event in the book.

The Integrated Curriculum. 1992. Teacher Ideas Press, a division of Libraries Unlimited, Inc., P.O. Box 6633, Englewood, CO 80155-6633

- Adapt an event from the book into a news report or television program.

- Create multiple endings for the book.

- Write a description of the book in 25 words or less; in 50 words or less; in 75 words or less.

- Create interview questions for a guest speaker.

- Rewrite a portion of the book with students as major figures.

- Create a glossary or dictionary of important words in the book.

- Create a rebus story for younger students.

- Write riddles about events or circumstances in the book.

- Design a "Question Box" containing questions and answers about specific books.

- Keep a card file of all the books read.

- Print important phrases or quotations from the book on construction paper and post throughout the room.

- Set up a message center to send messages to classmates and the teacher about books read.

- Create a calendar of important events that took place in the story.

- Pretend you are a character in the book and write a letter to someone in your class.

- Create a fictional autobiography of a book character.

- Write a travel guide for someone who wishes to journey to the setting of the book.

- Write a travel itinerary for visiting selected places in the book.

- Create a want ad for something in the book.

- Write a horoscope for a book character.

- Create a scrapbook about important places, people, and events in the book.

- Write a ten-question quiz on the book.

- Create a word bank of words from different parts of the book.

- Write a picture book (or wordless picture book) about a significant event from the book.

- Play a game of "20 Questions" based on book characters or events.

- Conduct a debate or panel discussion on an issue in the book.

- Interview outside experts in the local community about some information mentioned in the book.

- Create a new title for the book.

- Make up a list of information you would still like to learn.

- Make a story map of the book.

- Design a trivia game using book facts.

- Create a scale model of a location in the book.

- Create a time line of book events.

- Calculate the amount of time between various events.

- Create bar-graph representations of sizes of characters.

- Measure distances on a map or globe.

- Design an imaginary blueprint of a building or house mentioned in the book.

- Calculate distances between places.

- Create word problems using distances between settings, sites, or other geographical areas mentioned in the book.

- Ask classmates to rank their favorite characters in the book.

- Study the history of book making.

- Create a budget to travel to a place in the book.

- Set up a trading post in the classroom.

- Create flash cards using illustrations from a book.

- Design a pictograph of book events.

- Create a graph or chart to record book data.

- Calculate the heights or weights of characters.

- Use a calendar to keep track of important dates.

- Create a family tree for a book character.

- Identify foods associated with different characters.

- Create an environmental guide to the setting in the book.

- Make a climate map of an area mentioned in the book.

- Trace the lives of certain characters.

- Create a display of different forms of transportation mentioned in the book.

- List important discoveries noted in the book.

- Build a scale model of a book character using clay or papier-mâché.

- Create a montage of different shelters from the book.

- Create a replica of a historical site.

- Compare the living conditions in different areas of the United States.

- Chart the environmental changes that have taken place over a period of years for a place mentioned in a book.

- Investigate the history of a particular area.

- Create an animal or plant scrapbook about species mentioned in the book.

- Create a display of different landforms in the book.

- Create a "Bill of Rights" for book characters.

- Identify ecological concerns in the book's setting.

- Create a chart of weather patterns for different regions mentioned in the book.

- Write a logbook on the climate of an area.

- Construct a "self-history" scrapbook.

- Turn part of a book into a series of cartoons.

- Create a political cartoon about a significant event.

- Make an advertisement for the book or story.

- Draw illustrations of each character in a book.

- Create a fashion magazine using book characters.

- Put together time capsules for different time periods.

- Establish a museum of book artifacts in one corner of the classroom.

- Create a pop-up book about one important event from the book.

- With chalk, draw the outline of a country on the playground.

- Make masks of different book characters.

- Create an original slide show based on the book.

- Study paintings related to the book.

- Make a papier-mâché head of a major character.

- Design a new book cover.

The Integrated Curriculum. 1992. Teacher Ideas Press, a division of Libraries Unlimited, Inc., P.O. Box 6633, Englewood, CO 80155-6633

- Make a "flip book" about selected events from the book.

- Design an original flannel board based on the book.

- Create a radio or television commercial to get others to read the book.

- Paint a large wall poster.

- Design and create a diorama of a significant scene.

- Create a three-dimensional display of artifacts associated with a story.

- Give a chalk talk about the book.

- Take photographs of similar scenes from the local community and arrange them into an attractive display.

- Plan a bulletin board of pictures cut out of old magazines.

- Design clay models of important characters.

- Design a transparency about an important event and show it to the class.

- Create a salt-dough map of a specific location from the book.

- Develop an exercise program for a book character.

- List the physical skills needed to climb a mountain, conquer a distant land, or navigate an ocean.

- Invent games (for example, "Continent Twister").

- Play games from different parts of the world.

- Create a "Question and Answer Relay" using specific book facts.

- Create a radio show about the book.

- Act out events from a story and videotape them.

- Design costumes for characters in a story.

- Pantomime selected events in a story.

- Create a cultural concert.

- Sing folk songs associated with the book.

- Schedule and plan a "Culture Day."

- Role play a confrontation between two book characters.

- Present examples of music associated with various characters or settings.

- Design a filmstrip for a book (special filmstrip kits can be obtained from education dealers).

- Give dramatic readings of a book.

- Select appropriate musical selections for an oral reading of the book.

- Create cassette recordings of related stories.

- Dramatize a section of the book for another class.

- Set up an auction of items belonging to various book characters.

- Make up a scrapbook of quotations from the book.

- Write your reaction to the book on an index card and file it in a recipe box. Encourage others to do the same.

- Set up a panel discussion among several people who have read the same book.

- Make up several newspaper headlines about book events.

- List the qualities you like in a friend. Which book character comes closest to those qualities?

- Create a job-wanted ad for one of the characters in the book.

- Create a "Wanted" poster for one or more book characters.

- Cut silhouettes of book characters from construction paper and retell the story to a small group of classmates.

The Integrated Curriculum. 1992. Teacher Ideas Press, a division of Libraries Unlimited, Inc., P.O. Box 6633, Englewood, CO 80155-6633

- Explain which book character you would like to have as a next-door neighbor.

- Write to a pen pal in another classroom explaining what you like most and least about the book.

- Look in the telephone book for the names of people similar to the names of book characters.

- Work with some classmates to develop and design a "Who's Who" of selected book characters.

- Set up a literary review panel of classmates who can read and recommend books to other students based on their interests, free-time activities, or hobbies.

- Set up a television-type news team to report on book events as they happen.

- Establish an awards ceremony for books judged to have the best characters, most colorful illustrations, or best design (for example).

- Take on the role of a book character and write an autobiography.

- Write a movie script based on a favorite book.

□   □   □

Reference List

Cooper, J. David. 1990. "The Proof of the Pudding." *Learning '90* 18, no. 8 (April): 40-42.

Fredericks, Anthony D. 1991. *Social Studies through Children's Literature.* Englewood, CO: Libraries Unlimited.

Huck, Helen. 1979. "No Wider Than the Heart Is Wide." In *Using Literature and Poetry Effectively*, edited by J. Shapiro. Newark, DE: International Reading Association.

Huus, Helen. 1975. "Approaches to the Use of Literature in the Reading Program." In *Teachers, Tangibles, Techniques*, edited by B. Schulwitz. Newark, DE: International Reading Association.

Shumaker, Marjorie, and Ronald Shumaker. 1988. "3,000 Paper Cranes: Children's Literature for Remedial Readers." *The Reading Teacher* 41, no. 6 (February): 544-49.

Stoodt, Barbara D. 1989. *Reading Instruction.* New York: Harper & Row.

INFORMATION PLEASE

■ ── ■

By providing students with many opportunities to participate in their own reading growth and development, you give them a chance to become enthusiastic rather than reluctant readers. A true student-based reading program is action-oriented; that is, it is both "hands-on" and "minds-on." When students understand that reading is not necessarily a passive activity, they will be more inclined to embrace it as a natural part of their lifestyle.

What follows are several process sheets for periodic use throughout your reading program. They are not designed to be used with every student for every book. Instead, they give you and your students some options for extending and promoting literature throughout the entire curriculum. As with the activities in the previous section, feel free to adapt or modify these process sheets according to the needs and abilities of the students in your classroom. While you should not plan to use all of them with every book, neither should you use them haphazardly. Matching the process sheets to individual students and individual books creates many means for extending and enriching your reading program.

Things to Ask Myself When I Read (Table 1, page 21). Students may wish to use the process sheet in table 1 as an individual checklist of their own progress through a book. The emphasis here is on self-monitoring and the development of appropriate comprehension strategies. This process sheet is set up as a checklist that students can use periodically throughout the year, perhaps three or four times. After a student has completed one of these sheets for a particular book, schedule a conference in which you and that student talk about the items the student has checked and about some appropriate strategies the student might use to facilitate comprehension. You may also choose to have students complete this sheet and enter appropriate comments and remarks in a daily journal or diary for review or discussion later.

Interest Inventory (Table 2, page 22). If you use the process sheet in table 2 with all your students at the beginning of the year, you will get a good idea of your students' varied reading interests and can select literature accordingly. For younger students, it may be easier to dictate the survey to them and ask them to mark the appropriate number for each item. The list is intentionally long so that you can modify or adapt it for your own particular needs.

It is also appropriate to use this survey at the end of the school year as well, so you can learn what changes students made in their reading interests, likes, and dislikes. That information would be valuable to pass on to the next year's teacher.

Rate On (Table 3, page 24). One of the most powerful motivational devices you can use in the classroom is peer pressure. Students like to read what other students their age and grade are reading. This can work to your advantage, particularly if students have some concrete way of sharing their mutual interests with each other. The form in table 3 provides you with that option.

Have students complete this form for selected books read throughout the year. Completed forms can be posted on a bulletin board or collected in a three-ring binder and kept in a prominent place in the classroom. When students are deciding on a new book to read, they can check the bulletin board or binder to see what their contemporaries say about a book. You may even want to consider making arrangements with colleagues teaching at the same grade level to have their students complete similar sheets and establish a multiclass notebook of recommendations and reviews.

Literature Logs (Tables 4, 5, and 6, pages 25, 26, and 27). Integrating reading and writing can be accomplished through the use of *literature logs*. These process sheets provide ways for students to record their thoughts about books as they are reading as well as upon completion of a book. In so doing, students develop a reflective record of the literature they have read and they can use this information in conferences with peers or the teacher. It is important, however, that students be frequently encouraged and stimulated to complete literature logs, not on every book but on a periodic basis. This helps reluctant readers reflect on what they read, rather than just get through a book.

Three different logs appear in tables 4, 5, and 6. Feel free to use any single one or a combination of the three, depending on the needs of your students. Use these to stimulate conferences and promote active dialogue between students and their classmates, students and yourself, or students and their parents. None of these process sheets should be merely filled in by a student and filed in a notebook—if a sheet is completed, it should be discussed.

My Reading Report (Table 7, page 29). The process sheet in table 7 provides students with a way to track and record the books they read during a selected period of time (week, month, year). These sheets can be kept in individual folders for each child or in a classroom notebook. It should be the responsibility of each student, not the teacher, to see that these sheets are completed and kept up-to-date.

On each sheet the student records the title of a book read and the name of the book's author. There is a space for the student to rate the book on a scale of 1 (low) to 5 (high). The section titled "Pages Read" allows the student to record the number of pages read in that book. It is not important for students to complete every book they pick up. In fact, students may choose a particular book, read only ten pages, decide it is not their type of book, give it a rating of "1," put the book back, and choose another book. Such a record also alerts you to the kinds of books students select and the need for helping individuals choose books more in keeping with their interests and abilities.

The final column is used whenever a book is completed. In this space, the student records the extending project or projects done after the book is read (see the previous section), whether a mobile, diorama, poster, play, collage, or other activity. As is emphasized throughout this book, it is important for students to select these activities on their own, thus ensuring the motivation necessary for completion.

Reference List

Barchers, Suzanne. 1990. *Creating and Managing the Literate Classroom*. Englewood, CO: Libraries Unlimited.

Table 1
Things to Ask Myself When I Read

Directions: Check off the items that you want to think about.

Before Reading

_____ Is this similar to anything I have read before?

_____ Why am I reading this?

_____ What's in this for me?

_____ Why is this information important for me to know?

_____ Will I need additional information to help me understand this book?

_____ Do I have any questions about the selection before I read it? If so, what are they?

Guided Reading

_____ Am I understanding what I'm reading?

_____ What is this text all about?

_____ What can I do if I don't understand this information?

_____ Can I use this information in another subject or area?

_____ Why am I learning this?

_____ Are these characters or events similar to others I have read about?

_____ How does this information differ from other things that I know?

_____ Why is this difficult or easy for me to understand?

_____ Is this interesting or enjoyable? Why or why not?

_____ Have I changed my mind about any ideas I had before reading the story?

_____ Do I have any questions about this story that have not been answered so far?

_____ What new information am I learning?

_____ What information do I still need to learn?

After Reading

_____ Can I write a brief summary of the story?

_____ What did I learn from this story?

_____ Where can I go to learn some additional information on this topic?

_____ What is the major point of this story?

_____ Did I confirm (or do I need to modify) my initial purpose for reading this story?

_____ Is there anything else interesting I'd like to find out about this topic?

_____ Do I have some unanswered questions from this story?

_____ What makes me think my understanding of the story is appropriate?

_____ Do I want to ask any other questions?

The Integrated Curriculum. 1992. Teacher Ideas Press, a division of Libraries Unlimited, Inc., P.O. Box 6633, Englewood, CO 80155-6633

Table 2
Interest Inventory

Directions: Here is a list of things students like to read about and things students like to do. Circle the number after each item to show how interested you are in that particular choice.

		Very much		Some-times		Very little
1.	**I like to read about ...**					
a.	adventures	5	4	3	2	1
b.	animals	5	4	3	2	1
c.	art/music/dance	5	4	3	2	1
d.	careers	5	4	3	2	1
e.	cars/motorcycles	5	4	3	2	1
f.	comedy	5	4	3	2	1
g.	cooking/food	5	4	3	2	1
h.	exercise/health	5	4	3	2	1
i.	famous people	5	4	3	2	1
j.	fashion	5	4	3	2	1
k.	foreign lands	5	4	3	2	1
l.	games	5	4	3	2	1
m.	history	5	4	3	2	1
n.	human body	5	4	3	2	1
o.	insects	5	4	3	2	1
p.	make-believe	5	4	3	2	1
q.	model cars/planes	5	4	3	2	1
r.	mysteries	5	4	3	2	1
s.	painting/drawing	5	4	3	2	1
t.	plants	5	4	3	2	1
u.	romance/love	5	4	3	2	1
v.	science/science fiction	5	4	3	2	1
w.	self-defense	5	4	3	2	1
x.	sewing/embroidery	5	4	3	2	1
y.	space	5	4	3	2	1
z.	sports	5	4	3	2	1
aa.	stamps	5	4	3	2	1
bb.	transportation	5	4	3	2	1
cc.	trivia	5	4	3	2	1
dd.	war/armed services	5	4	3	2	1
ee.	world events	5	4	3	2	1
ff.	other_____	5	4	3	2	1
2.	**I like to ...**					
a.	build model planes/cars	5	4	3	2	1
b.	collect things	5	4	3	2	1
c.	go camping	5	4	3	2	1
d.	go swimming	5	4	3	2	1
e.	go to the movies	5	4	3	2	1
f.	go to museums	5	4	3	2	1

Table 2
(continued)

	Very much		Some-times		Very little
2. I like to ... *(continued)*					
g. listen to music	5	4	3	2	1
h. paint	5	4	3	2	1
i. play a musical instrument	5	4	3	2	1
j. play sports	5	4	3	2	1
k. play table games	5	4	3	2	1
l. play with animals	5	4	3	2	1
m. read comic books	5	4	3	2	1
n. ride bicycles/skateboards	5	4	3	2	1
o. travel	5	4	3	2	1
p. watch television	5	4	3	2	1
q. other_____	5	4	3	2	1
r. other_____	5	4	3	2	1
s. other_____	5	4	3	2	1
3. I like to read ...					
a. comic books	5	4	3	2	1
b. direction sheets	5	4	3	2	1
c. encyclopedias	5	4	3	2	1
d. funnies	5	4	3	2	1
e. hardback books	5	4	3	2	1
f. junk mail	5	4	3	2	1
g. library books	5	4	3	2	1
h. magazines	5	4	3	2	1
i. newspapers	5	4	3	2	1
j. novels	5	4	3	2	1
k. paperback books	5	4	3	2	1
l. textbooks	5	4	3	2	1
m. television program guides	5	4	3	2	1
n. other_____	5	4	3	2	1

The Integrated Curriculum. 1992. Teacher Ideas Press, a division of Libraries Unlimited, Inc., P.O. Box 6633, Englewood, CO 80155-6633

Table 3
Rate On

Directions: Review a book or story you have read recently. Based on the following scale, rate each of the characteristics of that story.

5 = Very interesting
4 = Interesting
3 = O.K.
2 = Not very interesting
1 = Dull

Post this sheet to share with classmates.

Book Title:_____

Author:_____

Main Character	5	4	3	2	1
Supporting Character(s)	5	4	3	2	1
Setting(s)	5	4	3	2	1
Time Story Took Place	5	4	3	2	1
Beginning of Story	5	4	3	2	1
Middle of Story	5	4	3	2	1
End of Story	5	4	3	2	1
Author's Style of Writing	5	4	3	2	1
Other_____	5	4	3	2	1

Would you recommend this book to a friend?

Yes _____   Maybe _____   No _____

Why? _____
_____
_____
_____
_____
_____
_____
_____
_____

The Integrated Curriculum. 1992. Teacher Ideas Press, a division of Libraries Unlimited, Inc., P.O. Box 6633, Englewood, CO 80155-6633

Table 4
Literature Log—A

Name: _____

Date: _____

Title: _____

Author(s): _____

The best part was _____

_____

The worst part was _____

_____

The main problem was _____

_____

_____

The problem was solved when _____

_____

_____

Powerful words were _____

Words I didn't understand were _____

My favorite character was _____

My least favorite character was _____

An important character was _____

I didn't understand _____

_____

I laughed when _____

_____

I cried when _____

_____

I celebrated when _____

_____

I will never forget _____

_____

I would recommend this book to _____ because

_____

_____

_____

_____

Source: Suzanne Barchers, *Creating and Managing the Literate Classroom.* (Englewood, CO: Libraries Unlimited, 1990), 74.
Used with permission of the author.

The Integrated Curriculum. 1992. Teacher Ideas Press, a division of Libraries Unlimited, Inc., P.O. Box 6633, Englewood, CO 80155-6633

Table 5
Literature Log—B

Name: _____

Date: _____

Title: _____

Author(s): _____

Some things I already know about this topic: _____

_____

_____

_____

Where I learned that information: _____

_____

_____

_____

Some questions I have about the book: _____

_____

_____

_____

How I think the story will turn out: _____

_____

_____

Things I would like to know:

    About the main character(s): _____

    _____

    About the setting: _____

    _____

    About the main problem: _____

    _____

What I learned from reading the book: _____

_____

_____

What I still need to find out: _____

_____

_____

Where I can go to get the answers: _____

_____

_____

The Integrated Curriculum. 1992. Teacher Ideas Press, a division of Libraries Unlimited, Inc., P.O. Box 6633, Englewood, CO 80155-6633

Table 6
Literature Log — C

Name: _____

Date: _____

Title: _____

Author: _____

Before Reading

Why do I want to read this book? _____
_____

What do I know about this topic? _____
_____

What questions would I like to ask before I read? _____
_____

What do I think the book is about? _____
_____
_____

During Reading

What am I learning as I read this book? _____
_____

What did I do when I didn't understand something in the book? _____
_____

Will I want to finish this book? _____
Why? _____
_____

Am I finding answers to some of my questions? _____
Is the main character(s) similar to any other(s) I have read about? ___
How? _____
_____
_____

Table 6
(continued)

After Reading

Why, in your opinion, did the author write this book? _____
_____
_____

Am I satisifed with this story? _____
Why? _____
_____
_____

Can I write a brief summary of the story? _____ Here it is: _____
_____
_____
_____
_____
_____
_____
_____
_____
_____
_____

Would I want to read this story at another time? _____
What questions do I still need answers to? _____
_____
_____
_____

How can I find that information? _____
_____
_____
_____

Here's how the author could have made this a better book: _____
_____
_____
_____
_____
_____

The Integrated Curriculum. 1992. Teacher Ideas Press, a division of Libraries Unlimited, Inc., P.O. Box 6633, Englewood, CO 80155-6633

Table 7
Reading Report

MY READING REPORT				
Name: _____			School Year: _____	
Book Title	**Author**	**Rating 1-5**	**Pages Read**	**Project**

The Integrated Curriculum. 1992. Teacher Ideas Press, a division of Libraries Unlimited, Inc., P.O. Box 6633, Englewood, CO 80155-6633

PARTICIPATORY COMPREHENSION:
Processes (Not Panaceas) for
Reluctant Readers

Traditional reading practices tend to emphasize assessment over instruction. As Durkin (1978-1979) pointed out, evaluation comprises more than 99 percent of classroom reading instruction. These practices (what I refer to as *exclusionary comprehension*) force students to respond to a never-ending series of queries that often are designed simply to identify the one right answer (i.e., the preselected answer in the teacher's head). Typically, pupils are seldom involved in utilizing their prior knowledge, processing their own thoughts and ideas, or engaging in an active discourse with authors, classmates, or the teacher.

The concept of *participatory comprehension*, on the other hand, underscores and emphasizes the reader's purposeful involvement in textual material. Individual engagement in literacy acquisition activities is valued and encouraged as an intrinsic correlate of effective comprehension development. Readers who are provided with multiple opportunities to control, direct, and monitor their own comprehension growth develop personal strategies that facilitate understanding and stimulate enjoyment.

In brief, participatory comprehension is characterized by the following:

1. It is active, interactive, and reactive. Students are provided with many opportunities to use their prior knowledge in concert. Background experiences are constantly energized, forming the foundation upon which text can be interpreted. Young readers establish their own directions for learning based on what they know and what they want to know.

2. It champions a personal engagement with text. Children do not passively participant in responding to questions; rather, they manipulate text in terms of their own needs. Pupils are allowed to process information, develop inferences, activate appropriate concepts, and relate new information to old within their own framework of expectations (McNeil 1987).

3. It stimulates a sense of ownership (Beck 1984), or what I prefer to call an *investment of self*, in the reading act. Specifically, youngsters are provided with chances to assume control over their reading destinies, take responsibility for their own learning, and engage in metacognitive activities that facilitate an awareness of reading comprehension as an active thinking process.

4. It focuses on the reader, not the text. The reader manipulates text rather than the other way around. The reader sets the course for investigation based on self-initiated needs. Reading consists of an interlocking series of reader-generated expectations based on prior knowledge and the evolving meaning of a text (Leu and Kinzer 1991). This is in opposition to externally generated controls that push young readers through a maze of artificially contrived demands.

To foster a participatory approach to comprehension development, classroom teachers need strategies that encourage active goal setting on the part of students. The implication is that young readers are more willing to participate in the dynamics of their own reading growth when given opportunities to do so. The result is a rise in the number of eager readers and a decrease in the number of reluctant readers.

Following are four separate strategies you can incorporate into your reading lessons and classroom plans to promote active engagement in the reading process. Obviously, you will not want to use these approaches with every book that each student reads—youngsters need a lot of time to read simply for the sake of enjoyment and pleasure. They also need opportunities to meld their reading experiences with the experiences of other subject areas. Thus, these ideas are suggested as ways for you to help your students get more out of what they read by focusing on participatory processes that enhance comprehension development and further involvement with the reading process.

Student-Generated Questions

One of the major instructional goals of any reading program is to provide opportunities for students to take an active role in the reading process. By that I mean that when students feel as though they have some control over their reading progress and enjoyment, they will be more motivated to read and to read with pleasure. In so doing, a measure of independence is achieved.

When students begin asking questions about what they are reading, they assume one of the major roles of an accomplished reader. Good readers do not passively accept textual information; instead, they compare it to their background knowledge, integrate it into their schema, critique it in terms of their belief structures, and interact with it mentally. Such is the mark of an active reader. As Vacca and Vacca (1989) point out, two of the most important questions every reader should ask prior to reading are "What do I think this selection is about?" and "Why do I think so?" When students begin asking questions such as these, they begin to establish their own purposes for reading and achieve a measure of reading independence.

Unfortunately, students do not have very many opportunities to ask self-initiated questions. The typical elementary teacher asks nearly 400 questions each day, 80 percent of which are at the literal or factual level. Most students' questions are of the "May I go to the bathroom?" and "Can I go to the nurse's office?" variety; children rarely get the chance to ask important and relevant questions. Yet, my own experience with reluctant readers has shown me that when students are given sincere chances to ask questions and seek the answers to their own questions, motivation increases tremendously.

In a sense, giving students an opportunity to generate questions that have meaning for them is a powerful incentive for them to pursue answers in text. This is something we do quite naturally when we read the daily newspaper. For example, if we saw a headline that said "Government to Raise Taxes 20 Percent," we might ask ourselves questions such as "How will this affect my family?" "Will I need to get a second job?" or "When will this take place?" We would then begin reading that article to find the answers to the questions we had generated. In other words, we were motivated to read that article because we had a personal stake in the information it contained.

For the reluctant readers in a classroom, this means that when you provide them with similar opportunities to generate questions about text and pursue the answers to those questions, you give them a forum in which they can take an active role in the reading process, develop a level of intrinsic motivation, and interact with the entire reading process.

Several years ago, my Chapter I students and I developed a self-questioning strategy we called the *Student Motivated Active Reading Technique* (SMART) (the acronym was intentional). SMART is a comprehension strategy that provides students opportunities to become personally involved in both expository and narrative reading. Self-initiated questions and concept development underscore the utility of SMART throughout a wide range of reading situations and abilities.

SMART, which is appropriate for individuals as well as small and large groups, can be organized as follows:

1. A book, story, or reading selection is chosen for the group or individual to discuss. Paper and pencils are provided to record questions and thoughts.

2. The title of the book is recorded on the chalkboard and individuals or the group members are encouraged to ask questions about the title or the contents of the selection. All questions are recorded.

3. The individual or group makes predictions about the content of the selection. Students decide on the questions they think will be most appropriate for exploration and designate them accordingly.

4. Any illustrations found in the book or story are examined and questions are proposed. The initial predictions are modified or altered according to information garnered from the illustrations.

5. The individual or group reads the selection (either orally or silently) looking for answers to the recorded questions. New questions may be generated for discussion as well. As answers are found in the text, the individual or group talks about them and attempts to arrive at mutually satisfying responses.

6. The procedure continues throughout the remainder of the selection, first seeking answers to previously generated questions and then continuing to ask additional questions. Upon completion of the book, all recorded questions and answers provided in the selection are discussed. The individual or group decides on all appropriate answers. Questions that were not answered by the text are also shared. Students are encouraged to refer back to the book to answer any lingering questions.

7. The individual or group can participate in one or more follow-up activities:
   a. Can we write or tell a new ending?
   b. Would another title be more appropriate?
   c. How would the story be different if …?
   d. What would happen if …?

8. More often than not, there will be student-generated questions for which no answers are found in the text (my students and I found that between 60 percent and 80 percent of the answers to their questions can be located in most stories). Many of those "leftover" questions can be pursued in other resources, such as supplemental trade books, encyclopedias, reference sources, and the like. Any questions still remaining can be discussed in terms of their appropriateness to the book, their level of cognition, or their need to be restructured or even eliminated as inappropriate.

There are three essential points to keep in mind as you use SMART with your students. First, students will be reluctant to use this process for the first two or three weeks. This is simply because they have not previously been allowed to ask their own questions—they have become too teacher dependent. If it is true that teacher talk takes up about 80 percent of classroom time, then it should also be evident that individual students do not have a lot of opportunities to engage in oral discourse, much less ask their own questions.

Second is the fact that students will tend to ask the kinds of questions they are used to receiving in class. If you spend a great deal of time asking low-level, literal, or factual questions, students will do the same, because you have provided them with that model. On the other hand, if you consistently model high-level, creative, and imaginative questions as elements in your instructional program, students will tend to do likewise. In fact, it is possible to get a sense of the level of thinking that takes place in a classroom by providing students with a chance to ask their own questions. The kinds of questions they ask will reflect the kinds of questions their teacher asks and so demonstrate the predominant level of cognition extant in the classroom.

Third, the key element in the success of SMART is that the teacher slowly begins to take a passive role in the process; that is, you need to assist students in assuming responsibility for initiating *and* answering their own questions. Guiding students towards higher levels of thinking is a major goal of this strategy.

Active Student Questioning

Students in my Chapter I classes used SMART for more than ten years. They enjoyed it tremendously because it gave them a measure of control as well as a measure of success in becoming active and involved readers. As students used the strategy through the years, we also began to discover some adaptations and modifications of the original design that made the process more interesting and individualized. We decided to give these alternate activities the title *Active Student Questioning* (ASQ) (again, the acronym was entirely intentional). Here are some of the ideas students developed over the years:

1. Have one student take on the role of a character in a story. Direct other students to question that individual about actions or events that took place within the story. The role-playing student is required to answer in the voice of the character.

2. Divide a group of students into two subgroups. Direct both groups to read the same book. Then ask each group to develop ten (or other appropriate number) questions about the story to be answered by the other group (orally or in writing).

3. Select a paragraph from the story and write it on the chalkboard. Direct students to create five or six questions about the paragraph. Ask them to read the paragraph and decide which questions were answered within the paragraph. Encourage them to speculate on the contents of the rest of the story based upon the previous discussion. Also, talk about why some questions might not have been answered.

4. Ask a question about part of a recently read story. The student who answers that question gets to ask the teacher a question in return (also about the story).

5. Give groups of students the first two sentences of different paragraphs in a story. Ask each group to write as many questions as possible about their sentences. Direct each group to write a complete paragraph in which they answer the questions. Make comparisons between the groups.

6. Direct a student to read to you. Afterwards, have the student ask five questions about the story for your response.

7. Display an illustration from a selected story. Have students write as many questions as possible about the illustration (discussion beforehand may be necessary). Then ask pupils to write a short story that contains the answers to all the questions. This can be done as either a group or an individual activity.

8. Using activity 7, have students exchange pictures and questions and write a story in which they answer the questions of another person or group.

9. Have students generate a series of question stems (between twenty-five and fifty) to be recorded on index cards and kept in a box. For example, "Why did the main character …?" "How did the story …?" "When did the story …?" After completing a story, students can randomly draw one or more cards from the box and complete the question stem(s) according to story information. The completed questions can then be shared among all class members.

Metacognitive Modeling and Monitoring

One truism remains constant whenever we talk about reading: We can never see what is going on in the minds of readers as they read a piece of text. Although we can use several forms of external diagnosis to differentiate good readers from poor readers, we can never be sure of the internal strategies any reader uses (or chooses not to use) during the actual act of reading.

While that fact may appear daunting to some, it can actually be a blessing in disguise as we attempt to provide reluctant readers with effective strategies that give them some independence in reading. *Metacognitive Modeling and Monitoring* (MM&M) provides reluctant readers with an opportunity to "see" into the mind of a reader during the reading process. The teacher serves as a model of efficient reading, demonstrating for students the thought processes and mental activities used while reading. When struggling readers are made aware of the strategies good readers use inside their heads, they can emulate those strategies themselves. MM&M gives students an insight into the mind and demonstrates internal processes that can be used as they read.

In this strategy, you select a reading selection and begin to think out loud, verbalizing what is going on inside your head as you read. Because students cannot observe the thinking process directly, your verbalization allows them to get a sense of good thinking as practiced by an accomplished reader. Since you serve as the most significant role model for students in all their academic endeavors, your talking while reading gives them some firsthand experience with reading as a thinking process and demonstrates processes they can incorporate into their own schemas.

Mason and Au (1990) have outlined a five-stage process of how MM&M can work with reluctant readers. Initially, you select a piece of textual material that is short and contains some obvious points of difficulty (vocabulary, sequence of events, ambiguities, etc.). Read this passage aloud to students, stopping at selected points and verbalizing the thought processes you are using to work through any difficulties. This verbalization is essential because it provides a viable model for students to copy whenever they run into comprehension difficulties in their own reading. Here are examples of the five steps:

1. *Make predictions.* Demonstrate the importance of making hypotheses.

   "From this title, I predict that this story will be about a missing ring and a haunted house."

   "In the next chapter, I think we'll find out how the two twins were able to sail to the other side of the lake."

   "I think this next part will describe what the thief took from the dresser drawer."

2. *Describe your mental images.* Show how mental pictures are formed in your head as you read.

   "I can see a picture of an old man walking down a country lane with his dog at his side."

   "I'm getting a picture in my mind of a sparsely furnished apartment with very small rooms."

   "The picture I have in my mind is that of a very short girl with curly red hair and a face full of freckles."

3. *Share an analogy.* Show how the information in the text may be related to something in your background knowledge.

   "This is like the time I had to take my daughter to the hospital in the middle of the night."

   "This is similar to the time I first learned to ski in Colorado and kept falling down all the time."

   "This seems to be like the day we had to take our family dog to the vet's to be put to sleep."

4. *Verbalize a confusing point.* Show how you keep track of your level of comprehension as you read.

   "I'm not sure what is happening here."

   "This is turning out a little differently than I expected."

   "I guess I was correct in my original prediction."

5. *Demonstrate "fix-up" strategies.* Let students see how you repair any comprehension problems.

   "I think I need to reread this part of the story."

   "Maybe this word is explained later in the story."

   "Now that part about the fishing rod makes sense to me."

These five steps can and should be modeled for students while using several different kinds of reading material. As you read and model, allow students opportunities to interject their own thoughts about what is going on in their heads as they listen to the selection. Your goal is to have students internalize these processes and be able to use them on their own for all kinds of reading material. Here are some alternate approaches to MM&M:

1. Have students practice the procedure with a partner. One student reads a passage out loud to another and verbalizes some of the thinking taking place as he or she reads. The partner records those thought processes and discusses them with the reader upon completion of the story.

2. Let students read a passage into a tape recorder. Afterward, they can play the recording, stop at selected points, and tell a partner or you about some of their thinking as they dealt with the text at that spot.

3. Bring other adults into the classroom to model their thinking behavior as they read. The principal, secretary, custodian, librarian, superintendent, and other school-related personnel can all be used as positive reading models for students. Be sure to provide a brief inservice on MM&M for each reader before their presentation.

4. Invite students from grades higher than yours to visit the classroom and read selected passages to your students. Ask them to model their thinking as they read.

5. Designate a student "Reader of the Day" who selects a passage to share with other students and demonstrates the MM&M procedure. This daily event makes each student in turn a model for all the other students and validates the utility of this strategy for all readers in all types of material.

Directed Reading-Thinking Activity

The *Directed Reading-Thinking Activity* (DRTA) (Stauffer 1975) is a comprehension strategy that stimulates students' critical thinking about text. It is designed to allow students to make predictions, think about those predictions, verify or modify the predictions using text, and stimulate a personal involvement with many different kinds of reading material.

What is critical about DRTA is that students are provided with opportunities to determine the intent and direction of their own reading discoveries. When DRTA is used in a supportive classroom environment, one in which the teacher encourages and stimulates student involvement, student engagement is assured. Students find DRTA to be a wonderful opportunity to apply creative thinking strategies and personal decision making to all aspects of reading. Reluctant readers in particular discover that reading can be both a personal investment and a creative extension into all forms of children's literature.

DRTAs are guided by three essential questions inserted throughout the reading and discussion of a book. These are:

"What do you think will happen next?" (Using prior knowledge to form hypotheses)

"Why do you think so?" (Justifying predictions; explaining one's reasoning)

"How can you prove it?" (Evaluating predictions; gathering additional data)

Vacca and Vacca (1989) outline a series of general steps for the DRTA.

1. Begin with the title of the book or with a quick survey of the title, subheads, illustrations, and so forth. Ask students, "What do you think this story [or book] will be about?" Encourage students to make predictions and to elaborate on the reasons for making selected predictions ("Why do you think so?").

2. Have students read to a predetermined logical stopping point in the text (this should be located by the teacher before students read). This point can be a major shift in the action of the story, the introduction of a new character, or the resolution of a story conflict.

3. Repeat the questions from step 1. Some of the predictions will be refined, some will be eliminated, and new ones will be formulated. Ask students, "How do you know?", to encourage clarification or verification. Redirect questions to several students (if working in a group situation).

4. Continue the reading to another logical stopping point. Continue to ask questions similar to those previously used.

5. Continue to the end of the text. Make sure the focus is on large units of text rather than small sections, which tend to upset the flow of the narrative and disrupt adequate comprehension. As students move through the text, be sure to encourage thoughtful contemplation of the text, reflective discussion, and individual purposes for reading.

DRTA can be a positive element in any reader's interaction with books and other types of reading materials. It shifts the focus from teacher-directed reading to reading during which students are given opportunities to determine what they would like to learn and how they can best pursue that information.

Reference List

Beck, Isabel. 1984. "Developing Comprehension: The Impact of the Directed Reading Lesson." In *Learning to Read in American Schools: Basal Readers and Content Texts*, edited by Richard Anderson, Jean Osborn, and Robert Tierney. Hillside, NJ: Lawrence Erlbaum.

Durkin, Delores. 1978-1979. "What Classroom Observations Reveal about Reading Comprehension Instruction." *Reading Research Quarterly* 14, no. 4: 481-533.

Leu, Donald J., and Charles K. Kinzer. 1991. *Effective Reading Instruction, K-8.* New York: Macmillan.

Mason, Jana, and Kathryn Au. 1990. *Reading Instruction for Today.* Glenview, IL: Scott, Foresman.

McNeil, John. 1987. *Reading Comprehension: New Directions for Classroom Practice.* Glenview, IL: Scott, Foresman.

Stauffer, Russell. 1975. *Directing the Reading-Thinking Process.* New York: Harper & Row.

Vacca, Richard, and JoAnne Vacca. 1989. *Content Area Reading.* New York: HarperCollins.

Part 2
Bookwebbing Techniques and Book Activities

BOOKWEBBING: Using Children's Literature across the Curriculum

■ _____ ■

Providing youngsters with frequent exposure to good children's literature continues to be the focal point of a successful reading program. Children who have many opportunities to examine and explore all types of literature, particularly in a supportive and interactive environment, develop a lifelong appreciation for books and stories. An effective reading program offers students many chances to interact with authors and share those experiences with peers and adults.

Likewise, students who have been provided with opportunities to discover the universality of good literature beyond the reading curriculum develop a lifelong appreciation for books. Indeed, when children are given a chance to integrate literature into every aspect of their lives, they begin to understand its importance as a conduit of knowledge, wonder, and imagination. Making literature a part of each aspect of the elementary curriculum is a primary goal of this book.

The Integrated Curriculum is designed to offer pupils a host of interactive opportunities with children's literature. It provides for integration of popular children's books throughout the entire curriculum. Moreover, students are provided with a multitude of ways to extend their comprehension of all subjects through the wide and wonderful world of literature. In short, students are offered many classroom experiences that facilitate their exposure to and appreciation of a wide range of books and learning opportunities.

The goals of this book are based on several interrelated areas:

1. Interactive processes. Children provided with opportunities to interact with and actively extend appropriate books will sense the dynamics of literature as an extension of the reading program.

2. Active participation. Too often, children are exposed to literature in a passive context. The approach in this book is grounded in the belief that students can elaborate, extend, and expand the concepts of a single book throughout their daily curriculum. Pupils need to actively share their experiences and relate them to materials read.

3. Strategic comprehension. Providing learners with a chance to develop their own purposes for reading and to reflect on those purposes is at the heart of any successful reading campaign. This book recognizes that youngsters have the capacity to develop individual techniques necessary to effectively tackle learning tasks and that they can modify or adjust their perceptions throughout that process.

4. Motivation. Stimulating youngsters to engage in learning tasks and maintain a high level of motivation continues to be a major concern of many teachers. This book is designed to foster an interest in all learning skills so that performance and persistence are maintained in a variety of positive academic situations. Young learners develop positive attitudes about their abilities as well as about the materials they are using.

5. Divergent thinking. Students who are provided unlimited opportunities both to process and to interpret information will succeed in any learning activity. The activities in this book offer children many ways to move beyond the "right answer" into new areas of thinking and cognition. Students become engaged in a rich and enthusiastic learning environment that does not limit their possibilities, but rather enhances them.

This book uses a discovery approach to literature. It offers students a multitude of interactive activities with literature that will enhance and extend the entire curriculum. The focus is not on the development of a proper way of thinking, but on the multitude of learning possibilities students can use in developing an appreciation for good literature as well as an appreciation for the entire curriculum. When students are provided with opportunities to examine, process, and utilize literature in subjects such as reading/language arts, science/health, art, mathematics, music, social studies, and physical education, their growth as learners is tremendously enhanced.

Bookwebbing is a concept that extends a single piece of literature across the curriculum. It offers students opportunities to make connections between subjects, to extend and expand their learning into a variety of topics, and to promote reading as a universal subject. Through bookwebbing, reading is linked to and makes connections with all the other subjects in the elementary curriculum.

The focal point of bookwebbing is a single piece of literature. From that book a variety of activities and projects emanate, each related to a particular area of the curriculum. It is important that students be allowed to create and design activities in keeping with their interests and needs, too. Thus, it is important to lead students through some of the following steps—the same steps you can follow in designing bookwebbing activities for other pieces of literature.

1. Select a book most students have read.

2. List the title of the book in the center of the chalkboard.

3. Discuss with students some of the events, characters, or settings from the book.

4. List the names of other curricular subjects around the sides of the chalkboard (see the diagram on page 39).

5. Have students brainstorm for related activities within each curricular area. Each activity should extend and enhance the book.

6. Have students concentrate initially on generating a *quantity* of ideas; later you can emphasize *quality* ideas.

7. Let students work in small groups, with each group assigned one of the subjects of the curriculum, to generate an extensive list of possible projects.

8. After the master list has been created, provide students with an opportunity to select at least one of the listed activities and use it.

On page 39 is a diagram of a bookweb that you need to fill in.

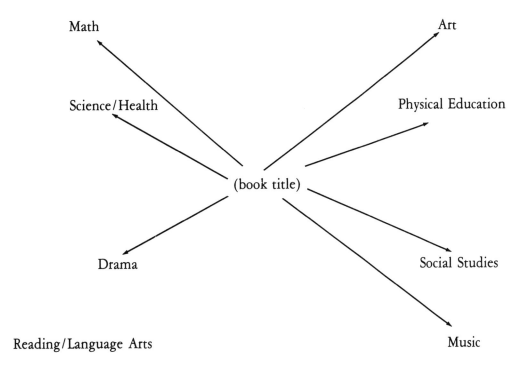

Math

Art

Science/Health

Physical Education

(book title)

Drama

Social Studies

Reading/Language Arts

Music

It will be important for students to select and participate in activities of their own design or choosing. As students engage in their self-selected activities, be sure to guide them to refer to the book and draw relationships between the projects they are engaged in and the ideas, themes, or concepts presented in the literature selection. In this way, you ensure that students understand the interrelationships that exist between literature and the other subject areas.

The following is an example of how one book—*Dear Mr. Henshaw* by Beverly Cleary—was developed into a multidisciplinary unit using the bookwebbing strategy.

DEAR MR. HENSHAW
Beverly Cleary
New York: Morrow, 1983

Math

1. Have students count the number of butterflies in a given area over a certain period of time.

2. Ask students to collect data on the size, dimensions, and weights of different types of trucks.

3. Have students calculate the number of letters Leigh Botts sent to Mr. Henshaw.

Science/Health

1. Have students construct a burglar alarm from wires, batteries, and bells.

2. Investigate the life cycle of butterflies.

3. Have students learn about engines and the nature of force, power, and movement.

Drama

1. Have students create a skit about a day in the life of a book writer.

2. Have students write a play about an imaginary truck driver.

3. Create a puppet show using some of the characters in the book.

Reading/Language Arts

1. Have students prepare an invitation for an author, truck driver, or caterer to visit the classroom.

2. Have students create a quiz show on letter-writing procedures.

3. Encourage students to establish a pen pal program with another classroom.

Art

1. Let students make a collage of trucks, semitrailers, and tractor trailers.

2. Have students make books in the shape of a butterfly and create their own butterfly stories.

3. Have students draw an illustration of the saddest part of the story.

Physical Education

1. Design an obstacle course on the playground that simulates the route the butterflies take to and from Pacific Grove.

2. Have students invent conditioning exercises for truck drivers.

3. Have students discuss how animals (e.g., dogs) can stay in shape.

Social Studies

1. Have students look into the history of book publishing.

2. Have students research some of the costs involved in truck driving or a catering service.

3. Have students locate and investigate all the states mentioned in the book.

Music

1. Play Saint-Saëns's *Carnival of the Animals* and direct students to imagine what instrument(s) might duplicate the sound of butterflies.

2. Ask students to choose some popular children's songs and rewrite the lyrics using facts from the story.

3. Have students select music that they think Leah would enjoy. Ask them to explain and defend their choices.

The process of bookwebbing provides students with a wealth of opportunities for extending literature far beyond the reading program and developing bonds between what they read and what they can learn. My own experience in using bookwebbing with students has been that it is enthusiastically embraced by reluctant readers and becomes a powerful motivational force in their academic pursuits. When students are given real chances to contribute ideas and to actively participate in those ideas, bookwebbing succeeds tremendously. In fact, I have discovered that there is no end to the possibilities that can be designed for any single book (as there is with convergent activities such as workbooks and skill sheets). Thus, divergent thinking is enhanced and motivation is ensured throughout the entire elementary curriculum with these literature "links."

AMELIA BEDELIA GOES CAMPING
Peggy Parish
New York: Avon Books, 1985

Summary:

When Amelia Bedelia goes camping, all sorts of interesting things happen. Try to imagine Amelia, who has never been camping before, trying to pitch a tent or handle sleeping bags without waking the others up. Her "adventures" are sure to tickle any reader's funny bone.

Critical Thinking Questions:

1. What would have happened if Amelia had pitched the tent so far it could not be found?

2. Would you like to have Amelia as a friend? As a neighbor? Why?

3. What would the story have been like if Amelia had gone camping by herself?

4. Would the story have changed if Amelia got frustrated and angry easily?

5. Why do you think Amelia behaves the way she does? Do you know anyone similar to Amelia (a friend, a family member)?

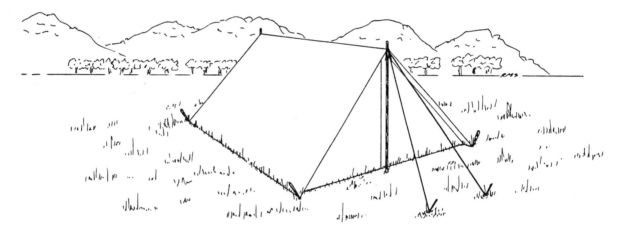

Reading/Language Arts

1. Have individual students make imaginary journal entries on an ideal camping trip, whether one they have really taken or an imaginary one. Provide time for students to share reasons why their trips were ideal.

2. Encourage the class to create and maintain a "running" list of all the homonyms they can brainstorm. Encourage them to refer to the list during writing opportunities.

3. Obtain a small tent and set it up in a corner of the classroom. Furnish it with pillows, blankets, and lots of paperback books and turn it into a reading center.

4. Students may enjoy creating a game of "Homonym Concentration" by writing homonyms on index cards and playing a game of "Concentration" with them. The rules for other card games can also be used for the homonym cards.

5. Challenge students to prepare oral summaries of the book in which they include four or five homonyms. Ask other class members to identify the homonyms in each presentation.

Science/Health

1. Have students set up a bird feeder. Cut out a 3-by-3-inch section from the side of a milk carton. Fill the bottom of the carton with birdseed and hang the feeder from the limb of a nearby tree. Encourage students to observe the feeder and the types of birds that visit it.

2. After a discussion of the four food groups, have students maintain individual records of the foods they eat during one week. Ask students to place each food item into one of the food groups. At the end of the week, discuss who had balanced diets and who did not. Two books to share with students include *You and Your Food*, by Judy Tatchell and Dilys Wells (New York: Usborne, 1986) and *Vitamins: What They Are, What They Do*, by Judith S. Seixas (New York: Greenwillow, 1986).

3. Set up a fish tank or terrarium in the classroom. These miniature "zoos" can be stocked with fish, turtles, lizards, etc. Have students keep notes on the inhabitants of these zoos. Two excellent books to help students create their own animal homes are *Pets in a Jar: Collecting and Caring for Small Wild Animals*, by Seymour Simon (New York: Viking, 1975) and *Beastly Neighbors*, by Molly Rights (Boston: Little, Brown, 1981).

4. Obtain a copy of *The Kid's Nature Book*, by Susan Milford (Charlotte, VT: Williamson Publishing, 1989) that contains a nature activity for each day of the year. Plan some daily nature activities for your students.

Art

1. Have students decorate the classroom as a campground. They may wish to bring in camping equipment to use as props or create their own illustrations of camping equipment for display in the classroom.

2. Encourage students to create a continuous camping collage. Direct them to cut pictures from old magazines and glue them to a long sheet of newsprint. More pictures can be added over a period of several weeks.

3. Ask students to design a perfect tent. What features should a tent have? What would make a tent more comfortable to live in?

Math

1. Amelia had to prepare enough food for three people. Challenge students to create recipes for all the people in the classroom. Bring in several sample recipes from a cookbook and have students modify the amounts and measurements to feed the entire class. Students can get easy-to-make recipes from *My Very First Cookbook*, by Rena Coyle (New York: Workman, 1985) or *Dinner's Ready, Mom*, by Helen Gustafson (New York: Celestial, 1986).

2. Ask students to predict the amount of space needed by a single person in a campsite. What elements need to be taken into account for each person's safety and comfort? How can those dimensions be expanded so that an entire class could go camping?

Music

1. Several recorded tapes of outdoor and nature sounds are available (check with your school's librarian or music teacher). Play one or more of these tapes for students and ask them to identify the objects or animals making those sounds.

2. Challenge students to create musical instruments out of nature things. Sticks, rocks, grasses, branches, and the like can be used to simulate the sounds of nature. Several can be found in *Make Mine Music*, by Tom Walther (Boston: Little, Brown, 1981).

3. Provide student groups with tape recorders and ask each group to record the sounds of nature in their neighborhoods, around the school, or in the local community. What similarities or differences do they hear or observe?

Social Studies

1. Contact a local travel bureau or American Automobile Association club and ask for maps or travel brochures of some camping sites in your state. Have students create various displays and collages of several locations.

2. Ask students to interview family members or persons in the local community for the reasons they enjoy camping. Why do people like to "return to nature"? Students may wish to combine their results into a report or chart for classroom display.

3. The National Geographic Society (Washington, DC) produces a number of videos and filmstrips on natural wonders and national parks. Obtain a copy of one of these productions (*National Parks: Playground or Paradise*, 1981 [catalog no. 51153] is suggested). Show the film and discuss the need for preserving our natural heritage so that future generations may have camping opportunities.

Physical Education

1. Take your students on a nature hike. Ask them to observe the flora and fauna of your local area and also to keep track of the exercise they are getting during the journey. What muscles are being used and what body parts are being stimulated during the hike?

2. Have students plan an obstacle course on the playground that would provide the exercise necessary to prepare for a camping trip. Have each student go through the course and record the completion time. Provide many practice opportunities and encourage youngsters to lower their times.

THE BEAST IN MS. ROONEY'S ROOM
Patricia Reilly Giff
New York: Dell Publishing, 1984

Summary:

Richard Best, the beast, is repeating second grade with Ms. Rooney. This story tells of his feelings about being retained and how he overcomes the stigma associated with failing a grade.

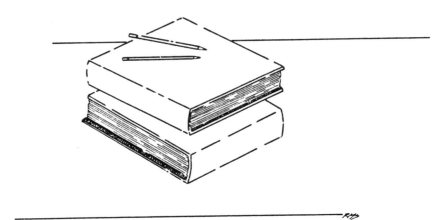

Critical Thinking Questions:

1. What events helped change Richard's attitudes by the end of the story?

2. What would a teacher think of a student who arrived at school smelling like a bed wetter?

3. What might his other classmates have thought about Richard (in chapter 8) if they found out that his misbehavior caused their class to lose the banner?

4. What suggestions could you offer someone who is repeating a grade?

5. How would you feel if you had to repeat a grade? How would you deal with it?

Reading/Language Arts

1. Have students brainstorm a list of all the benefits of repeating a grade. Have them create another list of all the negative aspects of repeating a grade. Discuss why one list might be longer than the other.

2. Have students write a letter to their parents or their best friend explaining why they have to repeat a grade. What should or can they say in the letter?

3. Ask one group of students to select several characters from chapters 1-3 and to role play them in the setting of your own classroom. Then, ask a different group of students to role play the characters in chapters 8-10. What do they note about the two presentations?

4. Have students rewrite the event on the baseball field (in chapter 2) from Drake's point of view.

Science/Health

1. Have students start a classroom aquarium. Bring in a brandy snifter, gravel, charcoal, fish food, and one or two goldfish (obtained from a local pet store). Put student teams in charge of maintaining the aquarium and periodically discuss the procedures necessary to keep fish alive and healthy. Students may wish to conduct some research in *Amazing Creatures of the Sea*, by Howard Robinson (Washington, DC: National Wildlife Federation, 1987).

2. Have students create a "Good Hygiene" bulletin board. They can cut out photographs, illustrations, and pictures from old magazines and assemble them into a display of healthy lifestyles.

3. Divide the class into several groups and ask each group to investigate the nutritional value of a particular school lunch. Each group can create a poster of the fat, carbohydrates, calories, protein, and vitamins in its selected school lunch. Ask them to determine the most nutritious lunch of the week. An outstanding sound filmstrip series on eating habits, exercise, and rest for youngsters is *Bodywatch* (Washington, DC: National Geographic Society, 1990 [catalog no. 30724]).

4. Have students make recipe cards for each of the foods mentioned in the story. Included could be recipes for tuna-fish sandwiches or homemade cookies. Next to each ingredient, have students note where it comes from and whether it is a natural product or manufactured.

Art

1. Provide students with opportunities to create their own original paper airplanes. Provide them with several different types of materials (typing paper, construction paper, onionskin, etc.) to determine which material is most efficient (this can be combined with a science activity). Have students determine which design best suits each type of construction material. Students might be interested in collecting ideas from *Easy-to-Make Spaceships That Really Fly*, by Mary Blocksma and Dewey Blocksma (New York: Prentice-Hall, 1983).

2. Bring in an old sheet and ask students to design a banner for their classroom that best represents who they are (as a class). Can they create an original logo or design to be displayed on the banner?

Math

1. Using the paper airplanes created in art activity number 1, direct students to fly the planes and measure the respective distances. Have students convert the distances into various units of measurement (meters, inches, yards, centimeters, etc.).

2. Take students on a field trip to the cafeteria, auditorium, or other large room in the school. Demonstrate how it is possible to calculate the seating capacity of a room by using multiplication instead of counting every seat.

3. Provide students with opportunities to "guesstimate" the capacity of various packages. For example, have them predict the number of raisins in a box of raisins. What attributes of the box and/or a single raisin will help them make an accurate prediction? Provide other opportunities with packaged materials for students to guesstimate.

4. Using geo boards or attribute blocks, have students construct an outline of Ms. Rooney's room. Can they predict or calculate the approximate dimensions of the room?

Music

1. Have students create a parade with a banner and a selection of percussion instruments. What instruments would be most appropriate to have in a parade (blocks, sticks, triangles, etc.)?

2. Challenge the class members to create their own class song. Have them select a well-known song (such as "Row, Row, Row Your Boat," "She'll Be Comin' Round the Mountain," etc.) and write their own lyrics for the tune. Students may want to vote for their favorite.

Social Studies

1. Provide the class with information and data on James Polk. Later, students may want to create a bulletin board display of important or interesting facts about Polk. Was he a good president? Why or why not?

2. Ask students to discuss why elementary schools are often named after famous people. Have students research the reasons for the name of their school. How did their school get its name?

3. Students may be interested in learning about the influence of airplanes on the history of this country. What were some famous airplanes and airplane pilots? How has the airplane influenced the development (political, social, economic) of this country? A book children will enjoy is *The Big Book of Real Airplanes*, by Gina Ingoglia (New York: Grosset, 1987).

4. Invite the class to discuss socially unacceptable behaviors (throwing spitwads, for example) and acceptable behaviors (helping an elderly person across the street). What are some behaviors students consider acceptable or unacceptable? What makes those behaviors acceptable or unacceptable?

hysical Education

1. Have students participate in a relay race as follows:

First leg:	Fly like an airplane
Second leg:	Gallop like a unicorn
Third leg:	Swim like a fish
Fourth leg:	Hop like a kangaroo

2. Have students brainstorm for all the games, activities, and sports they know. Ask them to arrange their list into several categories, such as team or individual sports, indoor or outdoor activities, physically demanding or quiet sports, and sports that exercise the whole body versus those that exercise only one part of the body. Discuss the importance of participating in a variety of physical activities.

3. Have the students play a game of baseball or softball and a game of kickball. Discuss the similarities and differences between the two games. Which one do they enjoy most? Which one is more difficult to play?

COMMANDER TOAD IN SPACE
Jane Yolen
New York: Coward-McCann, 1980

Summary:

Commander Toad and his crew travel aboard their spaceship "Star Warts" to a water-covered planet inhabited by the horrible monster Deep Wader. They must try to escape the jaws of the not-too-pleased monster.

Critical Thinking Questions:

1. What is your favorite animal? What is your favorite amphibian? Why?

2. What kinds of qualities must a hero have? Do you know any heroes?

3. Do you think there is life on other planets? What leads you to believe that?

4. Why did the author use a toad as the major character in this book? Would any other type of animal have been appropriate? Why?

Reading/Language Arts

1. Direct each student to write about another imaginary adventure the crew of "Star Warts" has on another planet. Provide opportunities for students to discuss their respective adventures.

2. Have small groups of students each create a comic strip version of the story from Deep Wader's point of view.

3. Set up a reading center in the room with multiple copies of all the Commander Toad books (for example, *Commander Toad and the Big Black Hole*, *Commander Toad and the Dis-Asteroid*, *Commander Toad and the Intergalactic Spy*, and *Commander Toad and the Planet of the Grapes*). Provide opportunities for students to read other books of this genre.

4. Have small groups collect a series of animal riddles from books in the school library. The class can put together a collection of the riddles they enjoy most and share their collection with another class.

Science/Health

1. A wonderful introduction to amphibians is the film *Amphibians and How They Grow* (1985 [catalog no. 30092]), part of the Wonders of Learning series produced by the National Geographic Society (Washington, DC).

2. Draw and cut out an oversized outline of a toad's body. Have students conduct some library research and locate information on toads specifically and amphibians generally that can be recorded inside the toad's outline.

3. Divide the class into several groups. Make each group responsible for collecting data and information about one of the planets in our solar system, to be presented orally to other class members or turned into a classroom poster. Two engaging resources for students include *The Planets in Our Solar System*, by Franklyn Branley (New York: Crowell, 1981) and *101 Questions and Answers about the Universe*, by Roy Gallant (New York: Macmillan, 1984).

4. Obtain tadpoles from a local pond or Carolina Biological Supplies (2700 York Road, Burlington, NC 27215; 919-584-0381) and set up a small aquarium in your classroom. You can also obtain the "Frog Hatchery" (an observatory, food, instructions, and coupon for frog eggs) from Nasco (901 Janesville Avenue, Fort Atkinson, WI 53538; 800-558-9595). Have students make daily observations as the tadpoles develop and record and illustrate their observations in a journal.

Art

1. Have students make hanging mobiles of our solar system. Tie several strings to a coat hanger and have students cut shapes from pieces of cardboard to tie onto each piece of string. Display these around the room. You may wish to obtain the "Star and Planet Indicator" from Edmund Scientific (101 East Gloucester Pike, Barrington, NJ 08007; 800-257-6173).

2. Cut the fingers off a pair of inexpensive work gloves. Direct students to turn each finger into a puppet representation of one of the book characters. These puppets can be used as part of a finger play or displayed somewhere in the room.

Math

1. Students may be interested in creating a display comparing the speeds of certain animals. Have students select the animals they like most and do some library research on the speeds of those animals. Their data can be recorded on a chart or graph hung on a classroom wall.

2. If possible, obtain several different amphibians (frogs, toads, salamanders) from a biology teacher at a local high school. Have students record their respective speeds by putting each animal on several sheets of graph paper and noting how many squares the animal covers in one minute. Discuss the differences noted.

3. Make up a chart indicating the relative sizes of planets in the solar system. The following scale will be helpful:

Mercury:	1/4"
Venus:	5/8"
Earth:	5/8"
Mars:	3/8"
Jupiter:	6¾"
Saturn:	5½"
Uranus:	2¼"
Neptune:	2¼"
Pluto:	1/4"

Music

1. Have students select a favorite song and rewrite the lyrics using events from the book. For example, to the tune of "The Farmer in the Dell," sing "Commander Toad and crew, Commander Toad and crew, Ho-ho off they go, Commander Toad and crew."

2. Play several examples of classical music for your students. Ask them to select the pieces that could best be used to highlight this particular book. You may wish to demonstrate by playing excerpts from the soundtrack to *2001: A Space Odyssey* (MGM Records [catalog no. MGL-513]).

Social Studies

1. Ask students to investigate the history of space travel. What were some of the more memorable events? What do they think will happen in space exploration in the next decade? In the next fifty years? A good book to read is *Finding Out about Rockets and Spaceflight*, by Lynn Myring (New York: Usborne, 1982).

2. Have students create and draft a travel brochure for the water-covered planet. Bring in examples of travel brochures from a local travel agency and ask students to create one especially for this book.

3. Have students plan a trip to a distant planet. What supplies and equipment would they need to take along? What forms of entertainment would they need? How would the space travelers get along with each other during the journey? Have them read *Nova Space Explorer's Guide: Where to Go and What to See*, by Richard Maurer (New York: Potter, 1985).

4. Have students draw maps of the water planet. Will the maps be complex or easy to draw? What features should be indicated on the maps for future travelers?

Physical Education

1. Lead students through a series of tumbling exercises similar to those experienced by the crew members on the inflatable lily pad.

2. Set up a "Toad Olympics" in which students do activities similar to those done by toads (for example, leaping [jumping for distance], sitting on a lily pad [balancing on a suspended mat], catching flies [catching balls]).

3. Divide the class into two teams and hold a series of leapfrog races around the room or on the playground.

ELMER AND THE DRAGON
Ruth Stiles Gannett
New York: Random House, 1950

Summary:

Elmer's cat informs him of a dragon who is being held against his wishes on an island far from home. Elmer saves the dragon and then the dragon and Elmer take an adventurous flight home.

Critical Thinking Questions:

1. Would you like to have a dragon as a friend? What kinds of things would the two of you do?

2. If you could change any part of the book, what would it be? Why?

3. Would you enjoy living on a deserted island? Why or why not?

4. If you could create an adventure with any kind of mythical creature, what kind of creature would you choose? How is your creature better than or different from Elmer's dragon?

5. Were you satisfied with the ending of the book? Would you want the author to change it in any way? How?

Reading/Language Arts

1. Divide the class into several groups. Direct each group to rewrite the story from the dragon's point of view. Afterwards, have the groups compare and contrast their versions.

2. Make a bulletin board display of a large tangerine tree. Cut out several tangerines from orange construction paper and direct students to create individual poems about characters or items in the story (e.g., the dragon, Elmer, canary, favorite food, etc.). Hang each poem from the tree.

3. Students may be interested in hearing other stories about dragons. Here are some to get you started: *A Good Night for Dragons*, by Roger Bradfield (Reading, MA: Addison-Wesley, 1967); *Sir Henry and the Dragon*, by Paul Cretien (New York: Follett, 1958); *Basil Brush and a Dragon*, by Peter Firmin (Englewood Cliffs, NJ: Prentice-Hall, 1978); and *The Laughing Dragon*, by Kenneth Mahood (New York: Scribner's, 1970).

4. Have students plan a trip to a deserted island. Ask them to prepare lists of items they would need to take with them on their journey. Ask them to consider the length of time they will spend on the island as a factor in choosing their supplies.

Science/Health

1. Describe the feeling the dragon had after standing in the cold water for so long. Have students fill several zipper-closure bags with water and place them in a freezer. Calculate the length of time until the bags are fully frozen. Have students periodically check the bags to determine the length of time necessary to freeze them. What could these calculations mean to dragons or people who stand in freezing water?

2. Two excellent films on cats are produced by the National Geographic Society (Washington, DC). They include *Cats* (1985 [catalog no. 51031]) and *The Cat's Meow* (1977 [catalog no. 51032]). Either one would be appropriate to show before or after reading the book.

Art

1. Invite students to create their own papier-mâché dragons for display in the front of the classroom.

2. Divide the class into ten small groups. Ask each group to select one of the ten chapters and develop a comic strip based on the events in that chapter.

3. Students can create dragons out of clothespins. Several clothespins can be painted green and decorated with wings cut from green construction paper and sprinkled with glitter. A magnet glued to the bottom of each dragon allows it to be placed on metal surfaces.

Math

1. Ask students to count how many tangerines the dragon and Elmer ate during the course of the story.

2. Ask students to determine the ideal measurements for a dragon. Provide them with the comparative measurements of lizards, dinosaurs, snakes, and the like and have students compute some appropriate measurements for a dragon.

3. Draw a large dragon on a sheet of newsprint. Ask students to take several measurements of various body parts and post them on a large chart. Then have students measure their own body parts and list those measurements next to the dragon's for comparison.

Music

1. Ask the music teacher to share songs about imaginary creatures such as dragons ("Puff the Magic Dragon" by Peter, Paul, and Mary would be a good example. The words and music to this song can be found in *Family Songbook*, music arranged and edited by Dan Fox [Pleasantville, NY: Reader's Digest Association, 1969]).

Social Studies

1. Study the cardinal directions and have students plot a flight plan to various cities throughout the United States.

2. Folktales and imaginative stories have been around for centuries. Share additional make-believe stories from years gone by with your students. You may want to use one or more of the following: *Hansel and Gretel*, by the Brothers Grimm (New York: Dodd Mead, 1984); *Jafta*, by Hugh Lewin (Minneapolis, MN: Carolrhoda, 1983); *The Legend of the Bluebonnet*, by Tomie de Paola (New York: Putnam, 1983); and *Saint George and the Dragon*, by Margaret Hodges (Boston: Little, Brown, 1984).

3. Have students make up a brochure on the routine and economics of taking care of a pet dragon. What food, medicine, or shelter would a dragon need and how much would it all cost?

Physical Education

1. Play a game of "Red Light-Green Light" with students, substituting the words "freeze" and "thaw" in place of "red light" and "green light."

2. Take the class on a dragon hunt on the playground. Pretend to run through some swamps, tiptoe lightly through quicksand, fly over a deserted island, and march through tall grass. Ask students to invent several different motions and exercises to do on the trip.

FISH FACE
Patricia Reilly Giff
New York: Dell Publishing, 1984

Summary:

Emily's unicorn was her lucky charm. When Dawn, the new girl in school, stole it, everything seemed to go wrong. Eventually, Emily learned that she did not need a lucky charm and that friends are more important than material things. This book is one of the Kids of the Polk Street School series.

Critical Thinking Questions:

1. What do you like most about your best friend? What makes a friend a "best" friend?

2. What kinds of things would you do to help a new student feel welcome in your classroom?

3. Do you believe in lucky charms? Why?

4. How would you feel if you were a new kid in your school? In another school? In a school in another country?

5. Is it more important to have lots of friends or a few really good friends? Why do you think so?

Reading/Language Arts

1. Provide each student with a block-style monthly calendar. Each day ask students to record one thing that a friend did that they liked. At the end of the month, discuss the types of things friends do. Is there a pattern in the events?

2. Ask students to write a short story about a lucky charm that gave them three wishes. What would they wish for? How soon would they use the three wishes?

3. Students enjoy reading other books by the same author. Here are a few more by Patricia Giff to get them started: *The Almost Awful Play* (New York: Viking, 1984); *Happy Birthday, Ronald Morgan* (New York: Viking, 1986); *Next Year I'll Be Special* (New York: Dutton, 1980); *Today Was a Terrible Day* (New York: Viking, 1980); and *Watch Out, Ronald Morgan* (New York: Viking, 1985).

4. Have students create a class poem about friendship in which each student contributes one line to the poem until the entire class has participated. Transcribe the poem onto a large sheet of newsprint for display in the classroom.

5. Provide several students with tape recorders and ask them to interview students in other classrooms about the qualities of a good friend. Bring the students together and discuss the ideas generated by the interviews. Are there any trends? Are there differences depending on the age of the interviewees?

Science/Health

1. Obtain a stamp pad, some paper towels, and blank sheets of paper. Take the fingerprints of each student in the class and display them in the room. Also, explain how no two fingerprints are ever the same. Help students look for the differences is whorls and loops.

2. Place a thermometer in an upper corner of the classroom. Place another thermometer in front of a small fan on a table or desk. Periodically, have students take readings from the two thermometers. Explain to them the reasons for the differences in temperature even though the thermometers were in the same room (hot air rises, moving air [wind] is cooler).

3. Ask a group of students to make a bulletin-board display on the four seasons of the year. Ask them to cut out pictures (of animals, sports, events, etc., associated with each season) from old magazines and post them in the appropriate places on the bulletin board.

4. Obtain some earthworms at a local pet store or bait shop. A worm farm (with worm bedding, worm food, and an instruction pamphlet) can also be purchased from Carolina Biological Supply Company (2700 York Road, Burlington, NC 27215; 919-584-0381). Allow the worms to crawl around on sheets of graph paper. Have students record the movements of the worms and their reaction to encountering different substances (water. alcohol, vinegar, etc.).

Art

1. Provide sufficient materials (cotton, papier-mâché, chicken wire) for students to create a life-size model of a unicorn. This can be a whole class activity with different groups responsible for different sections of the model.

2. Post a long sheet of blue shelf paper along one entire wall of the classroom. Ask students (over the course of several days) to turn the wall into a make-believe aquarium by painting illustrations of fish and other tropical creatures on the sheet.

3. Have students create a "character cube" using the characters from the book. Obtain a photo cube from a local variety store or photo shop and direct students to draw an illustration of each of six story characters to place in the sides of the cube. Each day turn the cube to one of the characters and ask one student to describe that character as a potential friend.

Math

1. Explain to the class that to bake a cake for the party, Emily's mother had to know how to measure the ingredients. Provide students with a simple cake recipe and ask them to prepare a cake for the class. Later they may wish to discuss the different measurements needed for the cake.

2. Ask students to calculate how many days the story took. Have them figure out ways they could prove their estimates.

3. Have students calculate the number of spelling words Emily had to write while sitting in the hall. How many did Beast have to write?

Music

1. Play the song "The Unicorn" by Shel Silverstein (New York: Hollis Music Co., 1962 and 1968) for students. (This song has been recorded by several folk artists and Irish groups.) Later students may want to join in and sing the song themselves.

Social Studies

1. Have students create a friendship book. Talk about the value of friendship and what a friend is. Then write each student's name on a separate sheet of paper. Over the course of two weeks, have all students write positive comments about the listed individual and why that person would be a good friend. The comments can be made anonymously but should all be upbeat.

2. Ask students to discuss the reasons for and effects of stealing. Why do people steal? How does stealing affect other people? If possible, invite a police officer or social worker to the classroom to talk about the ramifications of and punishments for stealing.

3. Have class members create a "Bill of Rights" relating to personal property. How should students treat each other's personal property? What should be done if property is lost? Post this Bill of Rights in the classroom and refer to it occasionally.

Physical Education

1. Have students run races similar to those run by Emily's class.

2. Have some students demonstrate Double Dutch jump rope and let everyone who wants to try it out.

3. Create a game of hopscotch by drawing a regular pattern on the playground and by writing the name of one story character in each block. Have students play a game of hopscotch—but before they can hop in a space they must give two reasons why the individual listed in the space would be a good friend.

HENRY AND MUDGE
Cynthia Rylant
New York: Bradbury Press, 1987

Summary:

An assortment of seven short stories about a very small boy (Henry) and a very large dog (Mudge) and the friendship they share while growing up. One of a series of Henry and Mudge books.

Critical Thinking Questions:

1. Have you ever had a pet similar to Mudge? Describe the similarities between the two pets.

2. What types of trouble would a big dog get into that a small dog would not?

3. What do you believe is the best pet for a young person? Defend your choice.

4. What are some of the things you would do if Mudge were your dog?

5. Would you want to have Henry and Mudge living next door to you? Why?

Reading/Language Arts

1. Have students rewrite the incident when Mudge gets lost from the dog's point of view. What was Mudge thinking about? How did he feel? Was he afraid?

2. Ask students to create their own dictionary of dog words. What terms and definitions should be included in a dog dictionary? Would there be different words for younger students than there would be for older students? Students can cut out dog shapes from pieces of cardboard and staple sheets of paper between them to create a "real" dog dictionary.

3. Have students talk about times in their lives when they have been frightened or scared. What events contributed to their fright and how was the situation finally resolved?

4. Have students write and create a guidebook on the care and feeding of dogs. If possible, have someone from the local ASPCA or Humane Society visit the class to provide basic information that can be collected into written form.

5. Bring in a collection of dog books and set up a special center in your room focusing on dogs. Here are some books to get you started: *Superpuppy*, by Jill Pinkwater and D. Manus Pinkwater (New York: Clarion, 1976); *Taking Care of Your Dog*, by Joyce Pope (New York: Watts, 1987); *Understanding Dogs*, by Su Swallow (New York: Usborne, 1978); and *A Dog's Body*, by Joanna Cole (New York: Morrow, 1986).

Science/Health

1. Take a nature walk and ask students to collect small samples of the flora native to your local area (be sure to warn students to take only *small* samples). Upon return to the classroom, have students arrange the items into an attractive collage or display.

2. Invite a veterinarian to discuss the diseases and illnesses of dogs. Discuss the preventive measures that help dogs stay healthy.

3. Have students each periodically record their individual heights and weights on a large class chart. Discuss with children the changes taking place in terms of their individual growth patterns. Have the school nurse discuss the average heights and weights for students at your particular grade level.

4. Have students bring in photographs of dogs they have as pets. What similarities do they note? What differences? Have students construct a chart or photo album that illustrates the variety of dogs and their characteristics.

5. Talk about the importance of exercise for both children and dogs. Have students discuss the various forms of activities that could be used by students and animals to preserve their health.

6. An informative video on dogs is *Those Wonderful Dogs* (Washington, DC: National Geographic Society, n.d. [catalog no. 51408]).

Art

1. Create a booklet of words that have *dog* in them: *dogwood, doggone, dogear*, etc. Have students create illustrations for the literal meanings of the words.

2. Have students create models of different varieties of dogs using pipe cleaners. Discuss the ease or difficulty of creating models of some varieties of dogs.

3. Using a large sheet of poster board or newsprint, have students paint an oversize picture of the dog in the book. When the picture is dry, have students write adjectives that describe Mudge in the middle of the painting.

Math

1. Ask each student to weigh and measure their pets at home. Direct students to bring that information to class and assemble it into a large book that records the information. Use the book to track the growth of all the animals throughout the year.

2. Ask students to predict the distance Henry and Mudge had to travel when Mudge was lost. Have students discuss the reasons for their various predictions.

3. Prepare a recipe for pancakes for the class. Direct students to modify the measurements of some ingredients to determine the effect on the overall recipe. Have students discuss the need for accurate measurements in recipes.

Music

1. Ask students to think of a theme song for this book. What popular tune would be most appropriate as background music when reading the book aloud to others? Ask students to defend their choices.

2. Ask several students to record a variety of dogs' barks. Have the class listen to the recordings and group them according to pitch (i.e., which dogs have high-pitched barks, which ones have low-pitched barks?).

Social Studies

1. Students may be interested in looking up some of the history of dogs. Books and materials on how dogs have benefited humankind over the years, as well as the role dogs have played in the history of this country, can be

shared and discussed. Find examples of heroic dogs. An outstanding book on the subject is *Dogs: All about Them*, by Alvin Silverstein and Virginia Silverstein (New York: Lothrop, 1986).

2. Visit a local pet store and obtain information on the prices of several varieties of dogs. Provide students with this data and discuss reasons why some dogs are more expensive than others. Encourage students to write to the pet store to ask them how they go about setting the price of the various varieties of dogs.

3. Have students create a poster on "What I Like Best about Dogs." Discuss all the possible benefits of dogs and have students list those items on the poster. Discuss whether there are any corollaries between what students like about dogs and what they like about their friends.

Physical Education

1. Have students prepare a tape recording (or videotape, if possible) on several exercises and activities that will keep dogs healthy and in shape.

2. Have students move around the gym floor as if they were dogs (on all fours). After an extended period of time, have students discuss some of the difficulties they had in moving about. Why is it easier for a dog to walk on all fours than it is for a human being? Have students decide on the muscles that would need to be exercised to make it easier to walk like a dog.

NATE THE GREAT AND THE PHONY CLUE
Marjorie Weinman Sharmot
New York: Dell Publishing, 1977

Summary:

Nate the Great and his faithful dog Sludge are out to solve another case. The only problem is that this one has a three o'clock deadline. Will Nate find the clues in time? What if he is too late? Is Sludge ready for the challenge?

Critical Thinking Questions:

1. How would the story have been different if Nate were unable to read?

2. What would have been different in the story if Sludge were a cat? A hamster? Another animal?

3. What would have occurred if the clue had not been phony and Nate really had been invited to a party?

4. How would the story have turned out if Nate had not been able to solve the case?

5. Would you enjoy solving cases like Nate? Why or why not?

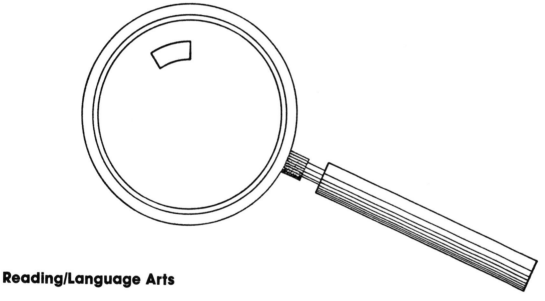

Reading/Language Arts

1. Have students create a secret code message to exchange with friends. They can use numbers instead of letters and send messages to each other.

2. Obtain other Nate the Great books from the library and have students create a special bulletin board display. Here are a few: *Nate the Great and the Fishy Prize* (New York: Coward, 1985); *Nate the Great and the Lost List* (New York: Coward, 1975); and *Nate the Great Goes Undercover* (New York: Coward, 1974).

3. Have students write a diary as though they were Nate the Great. What would they be thinking about this case? Any case?

4. Have students practice writing invitations. Write invitations to another class for a special presentation or celebration.

Science/Health

1. Have a police officer come to your classroom to explain how fingerprints are taken and used to identify individuals. Have students make their own fingerprint mural.

2. Have students make a pet bulletin board. Photos can be brought into class and arranged into categories (e.g., cats, dogs, fish; furry pets, scaly pets, feathered pets; mammals, fish, reptiles).

Art

1. Have students make up their own puzzles using construction paper. Cut sheets of construction paper into odd shapes and put into envelopes for other students to solve.

2. Have students create different printing objects. Potatoes cut in half, small pieces of sponge, and erasers cut into patterns can all be used as printers.

3. Using scraps of fabric, materials, pieces of wood, pipe cleaners, etc., have students create models of Sludge. Challenge students to create the most original, largest, smallest, or most accurate models of the dog.

Math

1. Encourage students to collect as many different types of timekeepers as they can (sundials, egg timers, alarm clocks, etc.). Discuss the similarities and differences between the various timepieces.

2. Have students create a sundial using a pencil, a sheet of graph paper, and a blob of clay. Have them place the pencil in the clay and set it outside.

3. A thorough filmstrip on time is *It's About Time* (Washington, DC: National Geographic Society, 1988 [catalog no. 30373]). It is a fine introduction to the subject.

Music

1. Collect and play examples of "detective" music. For example, playing the theme from *The Pink Panther* would be a good way to introduce this activity. What other kinds of "mystery" music can students suggest for the collection?

2. Have students record the theme music from various detective shows on television. Have students listen to the music and identify the instruments, rhythms, or themes that tend to predominate in this type of music.

3. Provide an opportunity for students to use their own instruments and create a musical theme for Nate the Great. This can be recorded and played prior to the reading of other Nate the Great books.

Social Studies

1. Using milk cartons, cardboard, glue, small boxes, and the like, have students create a three-dimensional model of a city. In what locations within this city would crimes be most likely to take place? Discuss why crime seems to predominate in some sections of a city more than in others.

2. Read other famous mysteries found in the library (Nancy Drew, Hardy Boys, Sherlock Holmes, etc.) to your class. Appropriate for both reading aloud and reading silently would be the Encyclopedia Brown books, such as *Encyclopedia Brown Sets the Pace*, by Donald Sobol (New York: Scholastic/Four Winds, 1982) and *Encyclopedia Brown Tracks Them Down*, by Donald Sobol (New York: Crowell, 1971). Have students locate the cities where all these stories take place on a large class map.

3. Invite a local newspaper reporter to your class to discuss how to obtain all the facts needed to report a story. What kind of research is necessary and how does the reporter go about obtaining that data?

Physical Education

1. Have students participate in a "Detective Race." Divide the class into two teams. At the end of a playing field, place two piles of clothing (hat, shirt, pants, shoes—all extra large). Have the first person in each team run to the pile, put on the clothing and run back to his or her team and take off the clothing. The next person runs with the clothes to the other end of the field, puts them on, and runs back to the team. The process is repeated until everyone has completed the cycle. The first team back wins the race.

PATTI'S PET GORILLA
Pat Rhoads Mauser
New York: Atheneum, 1987

Summary:

Patti wanted to bring something special for Show and Tell, but she could think of nothing. When the teacher asked her to share, Patti made up a story about having a pet gorilla named Bob. The class believed her and desperately wanted to meet Patti's gorilla. Patti's lie grew and grew until she finally told the truth about Bob.

Critical Thinking Questions:

1. If you were in Patti's situation, what would you have done? How would you have reacted?

2. If a real gorilla lived in your house, where would it sleep? What would it eat? What would it do all day while you were at school? Whose clothes would it wear?

3. If you could spend the weekend visiting Bob in the jungle, what would you do? What would you eat? How would you dress? Where would you sleep?

4. Why do you think the teacher did not tell the class that Patti did not really have a pet gorilla?

5. If you were a student in Patti's class, what would you have done? Would you have believed Patti's story about her pet gorilla? Why or why not?

Reading/Language Arts

1. Read the story to the point just before Patti tells the truth. Have the students predict how Patti is going to tell her class that she does not really have a pet gorilla.

2. In their journals, have students write about a time they were not truthful or about a time one of their friends was not truthful with them. Students should mention how they felt about that particular situation.

3. Ask students to bring in common household objects, such as a cup and saucer, a coat hanger, or a candlestick. Direct students to use their imaginations to develop each object into a fanciful object. Provide opportunities for students to share their ideas in writing or orally.

Science/Health

1. Have students view the National Geographic Society (Washington, DC) video *Gorilla* (catalog no. 50505). Have them make a list of all the characteristics of gorillas. How do those characteristics compare with the pets they have at home? Which characteristics are similar? Which are different?

2. Show students the picture on page 5 of the book. Have them list Patti's stuffed animals that can be seen in the picture. Ask them to describe the living conditions of each animal if it were real. What would it eat? Where would it live? Provide supplementary information from the library on each animal described.

3. Have students collect small bark and leaf samples from various trees in the neighborhood. These samples can be organized into an attractive display in the classroom depicting the various forms of flora extant in the local area. What animals will the flora support?

Art

1. Have students create a detailed map from their homes to the school. Direct students to use only symbols on the map, no words. Areas that Bob the gorilla would enjoy should also be included on the map.

2. Have students create papier-mâché or clay gorillas for display on a shelf or windowsill.

3. Have small groups of students create murals or posters of a jungle scene. If possible, place small puppets or stuffed animals in front of the murals to give the illusion of a three-dimensional exhibit.

Math

1. Have students make the following recipe to practice measurements and following directions. The amounts can be changed so that different quantities will result (for small groups or the entire class):

   Banana Roll-a-Rounds
   4 bananas
   ½ cup peanut butter
   ½ cup granola
   20 toothpicks

   Peel bananas and cut into 1-inch chunks. Heat peanut butter over low heat until soft. Dip banana chunks into peanut butter and roll into granola. Insert a toothpick into each chunk and freeze. Makes 20 banana roll-a-rounds.

2. Bring in several bananas and have students weigh and measure them. Before measuring, have students make predictions on the longest, shortest, lightest, and heaviest bananas. How do their predictions compare with the actual measurements?

3. Students may wish to create their own math flash cards in the shape of a gorilla. Basic math facts can be copied onto index cards cut into the shape of a gorilla and used for practice throughout the year.

Music

1. Ask students to listen to *Flight of the Bumblebee* by Rimsky-Korsakov. Ask them to imagine the scenes taking place as they listen to the music. What instruments create the illusion of bumblebees? What other animal sounds can be created with musical instruments? Does any instrument imitate the sound of a gorilla?

Social Studies

1. Provide students with information on the natural habitat of gorillas (maps of Africa will be necessary). Have students draw a map of a gorilla habitat, including where gorillas live and where they forage for food.

2. Invite a local zookeeper or biologist to your classroom to describe the location of gorillas in the world today. Encourage the visitor to discuss some of the threats to wild gorillas that are occurring throughout the continent of Africa.

3. Discuss the importance of telling the truth. Talk about why it is necessary for people to tell the truth and some of the consequences when the truth is distorted. Go to the library and research famous liars. Create a bulletin board of liars and contrast with a bulletin board display of truthful people and events in everyday living.

4. Have students look into the history or design of zoos in this country. How did they get started and what types of animals do they have? Some outstanding resources are: *Understanding Zoo Animals*, by Rosamund Cox (New York: Usborne, 1980) and *Zoos*, by Karen Jacobsen (Chicago: Children's, 1982).

5. A very informative video is *Zoos of the World* (Washington, DC: National Geographic Society, 1970 [catalog no. 51254]). Not only will students gain insight into the functioning of zoos, but they will also see how zoos are operated in different parts of the world.

Physical Education

1. Have students play a game of "Leap the Gorilla." The game is played the same way as "Leapfrog," only the students pretend to be gorillas. The game can be played in teams as a relay race.

2. Students can be provided with opportunities to practice their rope-climbing and swinging skills, pretending they are gorillas climbing and swinging through the jungle.

3. Conduct gorilla races. Divide students into teams of four or five and have them race across the gym floor on all fours, using both hands and feet (at least two limbs must be in contact with the floor at all times).

THE STUPIDS DIE
Harry Allard
Boston: Houghton Mifflin, 1981

Summary:

Stanley Q. Stupid and his family live a strange, mixed-up life. One night when the lights go out, the Stupids think they have died and gone to heaven, only to find out that they are still at home in their living room.

Critical Thinking Questions:

1. Do you think it would be interesting to be a member of the Stupid family? To live next door to the Stupids? To have a Stupid kid in your class?

2. What is something really stupid that you have done? How did you feel about it then? How do you feel about it now?

3. What made this a funny book? Would you enjoy reading other stories about the Stupids?

4. Are the Stupids similar to anyone you know? What makes them similar?

5. What other kinds of adventures do you think the Stupids might have on a daily basis?

Reading/Language Arts

1. Have each student add a page to the book by writing about one more event in the lives of the Stupids. Students will also enjoy reading other books about the Stupids found in the library including *The Stupids Have a Ball* (Boston: Houghton Mifflin, 1978) and *The Stupids Step Out* (Boston: Houghton Mifflin, 1974).

2. Select sentences from the book and ask students to replace words so that the sentences describe normal events. For example, "The Stupids all had breakfast in the *shower*, as usual."

3. Divide the students into small groups. Have each group write its own "Stupid" story. Ask each group to present its story as a short play to the rest of the class.

4. Have students each read a page from *The Thingamajig Book of Manners*, by Irene Keller (Milwaukee, WI: Ideals Publishing, 1981) and express the use of good manners related to that page. Students can then create a brochure or booklet of good manners for classroom behavior.

Science/Health

1. Have students bring several varieties of house plants to school. Set these up in a miniature botanical garden in one window of the classroom. Discuss with students the care needed for the plants and how they can be adequately

maintained. If you are interested in obtaining an indoor greenhouse kit that reduces maturity time by 40 percent, order the "Crystallite Indoor Greenhouse" from Nasco (901 Janesville Avenue, Fort Atkinson, WI 53538; 800-558-9595).

2. Invite a representative from the local power company to visit your classroom and discuss the nature of electricity with students. The visitor should also emphasize the safety measures necessary when dealing with electricity. An excllent introduction to electricity is *Discovering Electricity*, by Neil Ardley (New York: Watts, 1984).

3. Students will be interested to learn that there are more chickens in the world than any other kind of bird. Divide the class into several groups with each group responsible for learning about one aspect of chickens (life cycle, uses as food, evolution, etc.). Some good books for students to read include *Baby Birds and How They Grow*, by Jane McCauley (Washington, DC: National Geographic Society, 1983) and *Inside an Egg*, by Sylvia Johnson (Minneapolis, MN: Lerner, 1982). When each group has collected its data, the information can be presented to all members of the class.

4. Have the class brainstorm all the places electricity is used at home, in the school, or in the local community. Which list is longest? Why?

5. Discuss with the class different ways of conserving electricity (turning off lights, using fewer electrical appliances, etc.). Be sure to emphasize the reasons and the need for conservation of energy sources. Two books they will want to consult are: *How Things Work*, by Neil Ardley (New York: Wanderer, 1984) and *Things at Home*, by Eliot Humberstone (New York: Usborne, 1981).

Art

1. Have students draw a poster of their family engaged in one or more "stupid" activities. Ask each student to identify common activities done by family members on a daily basis. Direct each student to draw illustrations of those activities in "stupid" circumstances or locations, such as eating dinner in the shower.

2. Ask students to develop a new dress for Mrs. Stupid. What other types of "stupid" materials could be used in the design of her dress?

3. Have students, in small groups, draw the floor plan of the Stupids' house. How might the entire house look as a set of blueprints (provide examples from popular magazines for comparison)?

Math

1. Have students measure the growth rates of the plants they brought for Science activity 1. Ask students to chart these rates and compare the differences in the growth patterns of various plants.

2. Provide students with paper plates, construction paper, paper fasteners, and glue. Direct students to create several different types of clocks that might be in the Stupids' house. How would these clocks differ from more conventional clocks?

3. Refer to the picture of pyramids on page 31 of the book. Discuss the geometric features of pyramids and other geometric shapes. What advantages does a pyramid have over other types of structures? What disadvantages?

4. Have students count the number of chickens on Mrs. Stupid's dress. Ask them to figure out how many chickens it would take to complete the entire dress.

Music

1. Have students collect examples of "stupid" music. Recordings by artists such as Roger Miller, Weird Al Yankovic, and Ray Stevens would be appropriate. Discuss the elements that make this music humorous.

2. Challenge students to take a popular song and create new lyrics that turn it into a "stupid" song. Begin with simple songs ("Happy Birthday") and progress to more difficult songs.

Social Studies

1. Invite a blind person to your classroom to discuss some of the difficulties and problems encountered in everyday life. Encourage the students to ask questions about the lifestyle of a blind person, not only in terms of how different it is from their lives, but also in terms of how similar it is, too.

2. Direct students to prepare a report on their family name. How did their family acquire that name? Has it any historical significance? How long has the family had that name? You may wish to share with students the derivation of your name, too.

3. As a follow-up to activity 2, ask students to create new family names for themselves based on personal characteristics, features, or hobbies. Challenge students to spend a day referring to each other by their new names.

4. Have students discuss the perceptions and feelings associated with family names. Do people make assumptions about someone based on their family name? Why?

Physical Education

1. Have students do stretching exercises. See if anyone can touch their toes to their nose.

2. Conduct "mower" races. Divide the class into teams of two. One student walks on his or her hands while another student holds the feet of the mower.

THERE IS A CARROT IN MY EAR
AND OTHER NOODLE TALES
Alvin Schwartz
New York: Harper and Row, 1982

Summary:

A "noodle" is a silly person. This book is a collection of six stories about silly, strange, and weird people. It is also filled with chuckles, chortles, and lots of laughs for young readers.

Critical Thinking Questions:

1. Why did Mr. Brown and the children stay at the swimming pool even though it was empty? Would you have done the same?

2. Would you want to go camping with Sam and Jane? What other kinds of adventures would they get into?

3. Would you like to have Mr. Brown as a next-door neighbor? Why or why not?

4. Do you think that Grandpa will believe anything? What makes you think that?

5. Do the Browns sound like anyone you know? A friend? A neighbor? A relative?

Reading/Language Arts

1. Ask students each to select a silly person from their own family. Direct them to compose a story (real or made-up) about a humorous or funny event that happened to that person or as a result of that person's actions.

2. Have a "silly" contest. Challenge teams of students to select one individual in the school (principal, librarian, etc.) and invent the silliest story they can about that individual (be sure to keep the accent on the positive side). Schedule time for groups to relate their stories.

3. Ask students to select one of the stories in the book and prepare a sequel. What other types of adventures do the characters in the stories have?

4. Have students create a make-believe dialogue between themselves and one of the characters in the book. Which character would they choose and what types of things would they be able to discuss with that individual?

Science/Health

1. Several students may wish to grow some of the vegetables mentioned in the book. Provide individuals with small milk cartons filled with potting soil, three or four seeds of various vegetables, and some gardening tools (toothpicks, teaspoon, etc.). Ask students to plant their seeds and tend their gardens over a period of several weeks.

2. Have students investigate the evaporation rate of water. Fill several containers with equal amounts of water. Place each container in a different location (e.g., outside in the sun, outside in the shade, inside on the windowsill, inside in the closet). After a period of time (several hours), ask students to measure the water in each container and arrive at conclusions for the differences.

3. Students can conduct another evaporation experiment comparing the evaporation rates of different types of clothing material. Various swatches of material (cotton, wool, etc.) of equal size can be soaked in water and placed in an outdoor location. After a period of time the swatches can be weighed to determine which one allowed the water to evaporate fastest. What conclusions can students draw from this demonstration about their own clothing?

4. Have various students investigate the growing conditions (soil, weather, water) needed by the different vegetables mentioned in the story. Ask small groups each to prepare a comparative chart that identifies the planting and growing conditions needed for each plant.

Art

1. Students could create a line of greeting cards that might be sent by characters in the book. For example, what kind of card would Mr. Brown send to a distant relative? What type of card would Grandpa send to a friend? Provide examples from a local card shop to get students started.

2. Have students create a story mobile. Have them draw illustrations of various characters from selected stories or cut pictures of story scenes out of old magazines. Each of these pictures can be hung from a wire coat hanger with a length of yarn. The mobiles (one for each story in the book) can be displayed from the ceiling of the classroom.

Math

1. Ask students to bring in several types of vegetables they have at home. Challenge students to record as many dimensions of each different vegetable as they can. For example, which vegetable is the longest, the heaviest, the thinnest, etc. All the dimensions can be recorded on a class chart and added to throughout the year as students obtain other, different vegetables from the supermarket. Discuss averages, range, median, mode as you compare the vegetables.

2. Ask students to locate the current prices of all the vegetables mentioned in the book. For example, how much do pumpkins cost? A bag of carrots? Radishes? Or, perhaps, noodles?

3. Challenge students to make predictions on how much water is needed to fill an average swimming pool. List their predictions on the chalkboard. Bring in a five-gallon bucket and predict again. Make several phone calls to local swimming pool construction companies and get their estimates. Have students discuss the value of estimates when dealing with large numbers.

Music

1. Challenge students to create a band using only vegetables as instruments. What vegetables would they choose? What kinds of sounds can be created with vegetables? Can they play a version of a popular song using just vegetables?

2. Tape record one or more students reading their favorite stories from the book. Ask other students to bring in examples of recorded music that could be used as background music for that particular story. What type of music would they select? Popular? Jazz? Rap? Country/western? Instrumental?

Social Studies

1. Have small groups of students construct imaginary maps of the community in which the Browns live. What roads, streets, and avenues should be included? What businesses and stores? Where would the houses be positioned? The final maps can be displayed on the bulletin board.

2. Some students may wish to talk with the school or public librarian, the reading specialist, or other teachers about the origin of folktales. Why have some folktales lasted for so many years? To what can we attribute their popularity? Some students may wish to ask family members about folktales they learned as children.

3. Ask students to create examples of some of the clothing illustrated in this book. Using small pieces of material, students can create facsimiles of the clothes worn by the Brown family. Discuss the similarities between those articles of clothing and the clothes students wear today. Discuss with students the relationships between clothing styles and social customs of the time.

Physical Education

1. Have students invent and practice several activities that would allow someone to stay in shape for swimming (assuming there was no swimming pool nearby).

2. Discuss with students the value of walking as a form of physical exercise. Invite students to join you over lunch hour or during recess to take short walks around the school. Students may wish to map out several walking courses and keep track of the time necessary to complete each course.

GRADE 3

THE BATHWATER GANG
Jerry Spinelli
Boston: Little, Brown, 1990

Summary:

Bertie's gang of girls and Andy's gang of boys were always at war. One day, during a particularly intense mud fight, the two gangs discovered, through Granny, that they could join forces to form a single gang with one very productive purpose.

Critical Thinking Questions:

1. In the story, Damaris's mother is described as a flower child. What do you think a flower child is and how do you think they got that name? Ask your parents about flower children.

2. Bertie created a platform that listed the beliefs of her gang. What items would you include in your list of beliefs? Why are these things important to you?

3. Bertie's and Andy's gangs are rather mean to each other while they are at war. What are some tricks that could have been used instead of the one in the book?

4. Why do you think Granny did not feel that gangs were bad, as Damaris's mother did?

5. What would have happened between Bertie's gang and Andy's gang if it had never started raining? Would the mud hole have formed? Would Granny have started the Bathwater Gang?

Reading/Language Arts

1. While reading the story out loud to students, stop at the part where Damaris begins to rinse off the unknown person. Have students write, in twenty-five words or less, who they think the individual is. Ask them to pinpoint any story clues that led them to their prediction.

2. Appoint several students in the class as newspaper reporters. Ask the reporters to interview several students throughout the school on the advantages and disadvantages of membership in a single-sex group, club, or team. What differences do the reporters note in the responses of girls versus those of boys? Can they draw any conclusions? The results of the interviews can be written up in the form of a newsletter and distributed to all class members.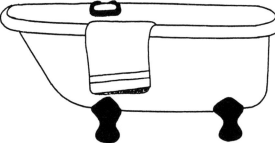

3. Have the students re-create one of the scenes in the book and develop it into a skit. The skit can be presented to another class or group of students. Afterward, have students discuss the advantages of working together as a team to produce an event or production.

4. Have students write to a pen pal in another classroom (make prior arrangements with a colleague) concerning the events and situations they enjoyed most in the book. Have each student invite the pen pal to respond with questions about the book to be answered in subsequent letters.

Science/Health

1. Ask students to collect samples of various kinds of soil from around the local community (four or more different soils would be ideal). Place an equal amount of each soil in plastic cups and pour identical amounts of water in each. Have students observe the results and make predictions as to which soil would be best to use in a mud fight. Which soil would be best to use with new plants? Which soil would be best to use with plants that need very little water? Students may wish to experiment by planting several different varieties of house plants in their soil samples and recording the growth rates of those plants to determine which soil is most favorable for plant growth.

2. Students are often fascinated to discover that there are different varieties of rain, from highly acidic rain (acid rain) to highly alkaline rain. Plant several bean seeds in plastic cups filled with potting soil. After the seeds have sprouted, ask students to water them with identical quantities of different types of water. To one quantity of water, add lemon juice; to another, vinegar; to another, a tablespoon of salt; to another, a tablespoon of baking soda; to another, nothing. Have students chart the results and discuss the implications of their observations.

Art

1. Have students create an oversize class mural depicting the battle at the mud hole, washing the pets, the pizza party, and other selected story events. Select several small groups each to be in charge of illustrating a selected event on the mural. The finished mural can be displayed along one wall of the classroom or in the hallway.

2. Obtain one or more refrigerator boxes from a local appliance store. Invite students to decorate each one as though it were a gang's clubhouse. These can be placed in the room and used as reading centers for free reading time.

3. Provide students with modeling clay and ask them to create several of the animals mentioned in the story. Students may also wish to create replicas of their own pets.

Math

1. Invite students to create their own word problems using lemonade. For example, if Bertie sold six cups of lemonade at twenty cents a cup, how much money did she make? Have students develop other appropriate problems.

2. Have students determine how many slices of pizza each girl could eat, since ten large pizzas were ordered for fifty-nine girls (figure on eight slices per pizza). Students may also wish to determine how many pizzas it would take to feed their class.

3. Have students determine Bertie's weekly allowance. Her allowance for the twenty weeks went to her parents to pay for the ten large pizzas; thus, how much money did Bertie lose?

4. Have students develop ratio and percentage problems to determine how many members signed up for Bertie's gang and how many actually showed up at the pizza party and at the meeting.

Music

1. Invite students to put together a collection of songs that pertain to water or bathing. (Some possible "water" songs include "April Showers," "September in the Rain," and "I'm Forever Blowing Bubbles," all of which can be found in *Family Songbook*, music arranged and edited by Dan Fox [Pleasantville, NY: Reader's Digest Association, 1969].) What songs do students sing at home or at camp that include water? What songs have they heard on the radio or television that have a water theme? Students may wish to interview adults about "water" songs that can be added to the collection. New songs can be invented and included, too.

Social Studies

1. Discuss with students reasons why people like to belong to groups or gangs. Why are individuals comfortable in belonging to an organization with other people? What benefits are there for the individual? Ask students to list all the "gangs" they belong to (the class, the school, their family, Scouts, a sports team, etc.). Which gangs seem to attract the most members? Why?

2. Ask students to design a community map of the area Bertie lived in. What services and buildings are in the town? What distinctive features does the town have? What geographic features are present? Students may elect to create two-dimensional drawings or three-dimensional salt-dough maps.

3. Ask students to discuss the qualifications necessary to become the leader of an organization or group. What leadership skills are essential to the smooth running and functioning of a group? Did Bertie have those skills? Have students put together a guidebook on how organizations should be run and how leaders should behave, whether they are the temporary leader of a classroom group or the president of the United States.

Physical Education

1. Create a "Question and Answer" relay. After students create a series of questions about the book, the questions are placed in two large containers. The class is divided into two teams. One team member runs to the opposite side of the playground, randomly chooses a question, reads and answers it out loud, and runs back to the team. A second person repeats the process until all team members have completed the course. The first team to finish and answer the questions correctly is the winner.

2. Students can play a modification of "Capture the Flag"; however, in this version the object is to capture a sheet of paper that has the other team's platform written on it (these will have to be prepared in advance). The gang that can capture the most prisoners and get the platform from the other gang wins the game.

CAM JANSEN AND THE MYSTERY OF THE GOLD COINS
David A. Adler
New York: Viking, 1984

Summary:

Cam can take "pictures" of scenes by using her mind; she only has to say "click" and she remembers the scene and can give exact details of everything she has seen. She gets involved in a burglary at a coin shop when she takes a picture of her friend, Eric, with the camera she made for the science fair at school. The thief sees her and steals her camera while it is on display at the fair. Cam follows the thief and soon solves the mystery of the stolen gold coins.

Critical Thinking Questions:

1. How do you think Cam can take mental pictures of something and remember every detail about it? Are you able to do that? Why or why not?

2. What type of punishment should Jimmy, the robber, receive for his crime?

3. Do you think Cam or Eric should receive a medal or reward for solving the crime? Why?

4. Why do you think Joan Cooper won the science fair for her entry "Soda, Sugar, and Teeth"?

5. Do you think Linda Baker's feelings were hurt because she did not win the science fair? What makes you believe that?

Reading/Language Arts

1. Have students mentally picture a scene or event that they all saw (for example, something that happened in the classroom in the morning or the day before). Then have each child write a separate description of that event or scene. Have students share their descriptions and discuss the similarities and differences that appear in the various essays.

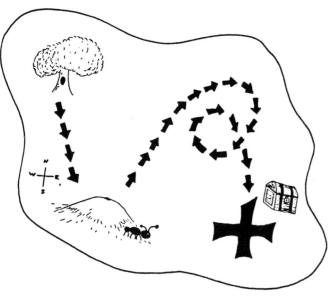

2. Before students read about the winners of the science fair, have them write a prediction of who they think won and why. After reading the results of the science fair, students should share their predictions and discuss why Joan Cooper won instead of Cam or the others.

3. Students will enjoy reading books in other detective series such as the Nate the Great series by Marjorie Sharmot (New York: Coward, various dates); the Detective Mole series by Robert Quackenbush (New York: Lothrop, various dates); and the Big Max series by Kim Platt (New York: Harper, various dates).

4. Another Cam Jansen mystery students will enjoy is *Cam Jansen and the Mystery of the Stolen Corn Popper*, by David A. Adler (New York: Viking, 1986).

Science/Health

1. Students may be interested in holding a classroom science fair in which every student in the class submits an entry. A teacher resource that focuses on a process approach to science-fair projects is *The Complete Science Fair Handbook*, by Anthony D. Fredericks and Isaac Asimov (Glenview, IL: Scott, Foresman, 1990).

2. If possible, bring in an old camera to take apart and show students the inner workings of a camera. You may wish to invite a local photographer or camera store employee to visit your classroom to explain how cameras work.

3. Ask students to keep track of all the sweet or sugared items they ingest in one twenty-four-hour period. Ask them to record the sugar content of their breakfast cereal, the snacks they have at lunch, and the dessert eaten at dinner. They may need to check calorie or diet books for approximate levels. Chart the results and determine which foods have the highest sugar content (the results may be surprising).

Art

1. If the students were Mr. Collins, how would they design their "Grand Opening" sign for the coin shop? Provide students with appropriate art materials and ask them to design several signs for the shop.

2. If students were campaigning for public office, what would their campaign buttons look like? Encourage each child to make an oversized campaign button from a paper plate. What designs or slogans would be included?

3. Ask students to collect several examples of comic strips from the daily newspaper. Erase the dialogue in the balloons in each strip and place these altered strips in a large box. Ask students to select one or more, create some dialogue that relates to the story, and insert that dialogue into the balloons of a comic strip.

Math

1. Students may set up a facsimile grocery store in the classroom. Various unopened or unused items can be brought from home (get permission first) and set up along a shelf or displayed on desks. Provide each student with a given amount of play money and invite them to get as many items as they can with that amount of money.

2. Read *Alexander, Who Used to Be Rich Last Sunday*, by Judith Viorst (New York: Atheneum, 1978) to the class. Ask one or more class members to keep track on the chalkboard of the different steps that eventually led to the total disappearance of Alexander's money. This can be recorded as a continuous subtraction problem during the reading of the book.

Music

1. Invite several Girl Scouts to your room to sing the Girl Scout song "Silver and Gold." Ask students to discuss the implications of that song and why those two precious metals were included in the song.

Social Studies

1. Invite a local banker to your class to discuss the nature of currency. Students should prepare several questions before the visit. The speaker can explain how coins are minted, how long they stay in circulation, what they are made from, and discontinued coins.

2. Invite a criminologist from a local college to visit the classroom to discuss how crimes are solved. What type of tools or materials do modern crime fighters have at their disposal to solve crimes? The visitor may wish to bring some tools of the trade for display and discussion.

3. Take students on a field trip to a local courthouse. Discuss the various activities that take place in a courthouse. If possible, have students watch a trial and later discuss some of the courtroom actions. How do they compare with what students have seen on television?

Physical Education

1. Create a treasure map (with chocolate gold coins as the treasure). Have students go through an obstacle course or orienteering course to locate the hidden treasure.

THE CHOCOLATE TOUCH
Patrick S. Catling
New York: Bantam Books, 1981

Summary:

John Midas loved chocolate more than anything else in the world! That is, until he discovered his chocolate touch. Now the word *chocolate* has a whole new meaning for him and he has to decide if chocolate is the best food in the world after all.

Critical Thinking Questions:

1. How does it feel to be humiliated? Cite an example of when you have been humiliated and what you did about it?

2. Is it important always to be honest? Are there times when it is all right to be just a little dishonest? When would you be just a little dishonest? With your friends? With your family?

3. Do you believe parents get overly concerned when their children are sick, or should they be more concerned? Does it depend on the nature of the illness?

4. What would you do if you could have the "chocolate touch" for just one day? For just one hour? For just one minute?

5. If you could have any magical power at all, what would it be? How long would you want to have that power?

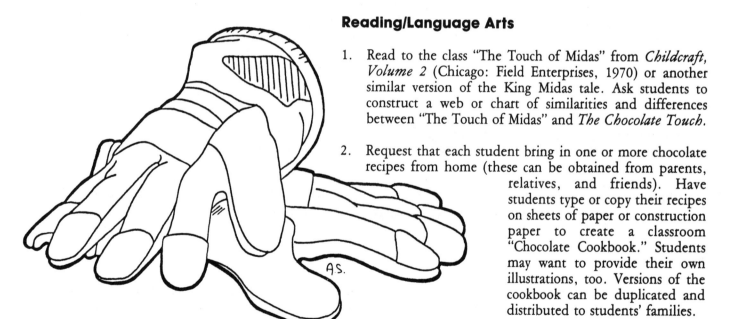

Reading/Language Arts

1. Read to the class "The Touch of Midas" from *Childcraft, Volume 2* (Chicago: Field Enterprises, 1970) or another similar version of the King Midas tale. Ask students to construct a web or chart of similarities and differences between "The Touch of Midas" and *The Chocolate Touch.*

2. Request that each student bring in one or more chocolate recipes from home (these can be obtained from parents, relatives, and friends). Have students type or copy their recipes on sheets of paper or construction paper to create a classroom "Chocolate Cookbook." Students may want to provide their own illustrations, too. Versions of the cookbook can be duplicated and distributed to students' families.

3. Have one or more students volunteer to read the poem, "Don't Eat the Food That Is Sitting on Your Plate" from *Noises From under the Rug: The Barry Louis Polisar Song Book* (Baltimore, MD: Rainbow Morning Music, 1985). Discuss the implications of that poem and its relationship to the book.

4. Have small groups of students each make up a magazine advertisement for their favorite or an original chocolate product. Have students find sample ads from several magazines from the library before having them create an original one. The finished products can be displayed throughout the room or collected in a special scrapbook.

Science/Health

1. Create a columnar wall chart. Title each column with the name of one of the four basic food groups. As students find the names of foods in the story, ask them to write those names in the correct columns. Encourage students to add the names of some of their favorite (or not-so-favorite) foods into the proper columns, too.

2. Check in your local Yellow Pages for confectioners or candy stores. Ask a local candy maker to visit your class to explain the processes used to turn cocoa beans into chocolate. Use the library to research and trace the journey of cocoa beans from their tropical sources to their final form as milk chocolate. Later, students can prepare this information in the form of a chart or graph.

3. Challenge students to plan meals for one day using only foods that they list as their favorites. Are all the food groups represented in the class's final list? Can nutritious and satisfying meals be created for breakfast, lunch, and dinner with the foods students enjoy? Students may wish to duplicate their final menus and share them with parents.

4. Cocoa beans are a product of the tropical areas of South America. Read the students *The Great Kapok Tree*, by Lynn Cherry (New York: Gulliver Books, 1990) or *One Day in the Tropical Rainforest*, by Jean George (New York: Crowell, 1990). Afterward, discuss the implications of thousands of acres of tropical rain forest being devastated each year. Have students investigate this ecological threat by writing to an environmental group such as the Natural Resources Defense Council (40 West 20th Street, New York, NY 10011) or National Wildlife Federation (1400 16th Street, Washington, DC 20036). The information gathered can be illustrated and charted for all class members.

Art

1. Ask students to invent and design an appropriate comic strip for this book. The strip can be a summarization of the major events in the book or a pictorial representation of students' favorite sections.

2. Have students create a three-dimensional collage of important artifacts mentioned in the story. Have students collect items from home to be affixed to a large piece of cardboard and developed into an oversized display. Next to each artifact, students can designate the book page on which it is first mentioned.

Math

1. Ask students to select one of the recipes brought in for activity 2 in "Reading/Language Arts." Have students double and triple the recipe quantities. They may halve the quantities, too. These restructured recipes can be posted on the bulletin board next to the originals.

2. Ask the students to solve the four math problems on the test given by Miss Pimsole to her class.

3. Visit a local candy store and obtain half-pound samples of five or more different varieties of wrapped candy. Ask students to count out the number of items in each half-pound sample. How can they account for the differences in quantities? Students can then do some comparative weighing, using a balance scale to determine the comparative weights of one type of candy versus another (encourage students to make some predictions beforehand).

4. When visiting the candy store, obtain a price list for several different types of candy. Tell students that they each have been given five dollars and must select four different types of candy from the price list. Their objective is to come as close as possible to the five-dollar limit without going over it. Later, have students devise their own problems using the list.

Music

1. Cocoa is an important crop from South America. Your students may enjoy creating their own musical instruments similar to those used in Brazil, Argentina, and other South American countries. Examples of primitive instruments can be found in *Make Mine Music*, by Tom Walther (Boston: Little, Brown, 1981).

Social Studies

1. Students may be interested in the history of chocolate in this country. Write to Hershey's Chocolate World (Chocolate Avenue, Hershey, PA 17033) to obtain information on the historical antecedents of chocolate making in this country.

2. Chocolate comes in many different varieties. Ask students to look into the economics of chocolate. Tell them to check with local confectioners to determine how chocolate is priced. Why are some forms of chocolate more expensive than others?

3. Show the video *South America* (Washington, DC: National Geographic Society, 1991 [catalog no. 51441]). Discuss with students the geography and climate of South America and why it is the world's leading producer of cocoa beans.

Physical Education

1. Play "Blindman's Bluff," "Grandmother's Footsteps," and "Fox and Geese" with students, as the children played in the book.

2. Challenge students to create their own "chocolate" games. For example, invent "Chocolate Kickball," in which each batter must name two different forms of chocolate before coming up to bat, or "Chocolate Jump Rope" in which students modify favorite jump-rope rhymes using chocolate words or events from the story.

ENCYCLOPEDIA BROWN AND THE CASE
OF THE MIDNIGHT VISITOR
Donald J. Sobol
New York: Bantam Books, 1987

Summary:

Leroy Brown, known to his friends as "Encyclopedia," is on the trail of several new mysteries. He needs to use all his deductive reasoning skills and problem-solving abilities so that justice will prevail. One of several Encyclopedia Brown books.

Critical Thinking Questions:

1. What rules would you want to change or modify in your family? In your school? In your classroom?

2. How can you improve your deductive reasoning skills? In other words, what do you need to do to become a better thinker?

3. What would you enjoy most about working alongside Encyclopedia Brown?

4. What are some occupations (other than detective) in which Encyclopedia Brown will be able to use his reasoning powers when he grows up?

5. What are some mysteries or cases you have been involved in that Encyclopedia Brown would be able to solve?

Reading/Language Arts

1. Ask students to record daily events in their own lives that they believe would be useful to a detective trying to solve a case. If you wish, create an imaginary mystery with several selected events. Have students list in their journals facts from each day that would be useful in solving the mystery.

2. Each chapter relates a different mystery story to be solved. Have students, in small groups, read each story and discuss possible solutions. Have the groups write their solutions and later compare them to the actual solutions in the back of the book.

3. Other Encyclopedia Brown books students will enjoy reading include *Encyclopedia Brown Sets the Pace*, by Donald Sobol (New York: Scholastic/Four Winds, 1982); *Encyclopedia Brown Tracks Them Down*, by Donald Sobol (New York: Crowell, 1971); *Encyclopedia Brown Takes the Case*, by Donald Sobol (New York: Lodestar, 1973); and *Encyclopedia Brown, Boy Detective*, by Donald Sobol (New York: Lodestar, 1963).

Science/Health

1. In "The Case of the Red Sweater," a girl finds a human skull. Have students research the human skeleton. What holds bones together? How many large bones are in the human body? How does the human skeleton compare

with that of a dog? A gorilla? A lizard? What bones are in the head? Two outstanding books are *The Human Body*, by Jonathan Miller (New York: Viking, 1983) and *Blood and Guts: A Working Guide to Your Own Insides*, by Linda Allison (Boston: Little, Brown, 1976).

2. If students have small, caged animals at home, ask them to bring those animals to class for one to two weeks. Ask each student to share the requirements for care and feeding of the pets. A large chart can be posted in the classroom comparing selected features of the animals.

3. Invite the school nurse to discuss first aid procedures. Ask the nurse to discuss the materials and techniques for simple first aid solutions. Before the visit, have the class compile a series of questions to ask.

4. Two fascinating videos from the National Geographic Society (Washington, DC) include *Where Animals Live* (1988 [catalog no. 51319]) and *How Animals Get Their Food* (1988 [catalog no. 51318]).

5. Some excellent books on animals include: *All Wet! All Wet!*, by James Skofield (New York: Harper and Row, 1984); *Whose Footprints*, by Masayuki Yabuuchi (New York: Philomel, 1985); *One Day in the Desert*, by Jean Craighead George (New York: Crowell, 1983); and *Elephants Can't Jump and Other Freaky Facts about Animals*, by Barbara Seuling (New York: Lodestar, 1984).

Art

1. Have students construct an Idaville artscape, including such landmarks as Seaside View, three theaters, four banks, churches, one synagogue, and two delicatessens. The artscape can be constructed from scraps of wood, papier-mâché, or as a salt-dough map. (To make salt dough, mix one part flour with one-half part salt. Slowly add one-third part water and squeeze the mixture until it is smooth.)

2. As in "The Case of the Hidden Penny," have students make plaster impressions of various coins. The impressions can be made in modeling clay or plaster of paris. When dry, they can be displayed around the room or used as part of a math activity.

Math

1. Have students create word problems using Encyclopedia Brown as the main character. For example, if Encyclopedia Brown solved ten cases a year for twenty-five cents a case, how much money would he make? If he charged thirty cents a case in the following year (due to inflation), how much *more* money would he make if he solved the same number of cases?

2. Have students list the titles of each of the stories on a sheet of paper. Under each title, have students decide on the types of mathematical computations needed to solve the crime (addition, subtraction, division, or multiplication). Discuss with students the reasons why more than one type of computation may be needed to solve a single case.

Music

1. Have students put together their own "Mystery Band." Provide them with an assortment of instruments (recorder, small drum, xylophone, etc.) and challenge them to create a "detective" tune or mystery show theme song. Discuss the instruments that create the most detective-sounding tunes. You may wish to record the theme songs from television detective or mystery shows to demonstrate the variety possible.

Social Studies

1. Ask students to assemble a time capsule containing clues about school life today, to be dug up in 100 years. If they could include only five items, which five would give the people of the future the most information about school life today?

2. Ask students to discuss the concept of citizenship. What does it take to be a good citizen? Relate their discussion to the story about the theft of the tennis racquet. Is being honest a part of good citizenship? Invite a local government official to your class to discuss the importance of good citizenship to the local community.

3. Have students discuss the write a "Bill of Rights for Kids." What rights should students have that might be different from the rights of adults? Should there be any differences at all? What would students like to see in a classroom bill of rights? If there were a children's bill of rights, and all students followed it, would Encyclopedia Brown be out of business?

Physical Education

1. Students may enjoy playing a modified game of tennis. Tennis racquets and balls can be used on the playground with a chalked or painted line instead of a net. Modify the scoring system so that it is similar to the scoring used in volleyball.

2. Students may enjoy participating in whole class tug-of-war contests. These can be modified so that the object is not to see which team can pull the other team over a line, but rather to see what combination of students on each team creates the most balanced event (each team pulling as hard as it can with neither team moving).

THE FLUNKING OF JOSHUA T. BATES
Susan Shreve
New York: Borzoi Books, 1984

Summary:

On his way home from the beach, Joshua T. Bates receives the news that he must repeat third grade. With the help of a kind teacher, Joshua tries to work his way back to fourth grade. Although he is teased by some of his old classmates, he gets the last laugh.

Critical Thinking Questions:

1. Why is it important for children to learn how to read? What might be some consequences if students did not learn how to read in school?

2. If you were Joshua, how would you have handled some of the situations he found himself in during the story? Would you have behaved any differently?

3. What do you think Joshua would have done if he had not passed his test? How would he have felt?

4. Can you define the word *friendship*? What does a friend mean to you? How important are friends?

5. If you could, what would you like to tell the author of this story?

Reading/Language Arts

1. Make arrangements with a colleague in a grade lower than yours to set up a tutoring bureau through which several of your students work with youngsters in another grade. The tutoring can consist of practicing math facts, reading stories, or working on a science project together. The tutors should maintain journals about their experiences to discuss in class later.

2. Divide the class into several groups and encourage each group to talk about what Joshua's friend should have done. Have each group share their decision(s) with the rest of the class. Did Joshua's friend make the right decision to talk to Joshua only behind everyone's back?

3. Have students write an imaginary letter to Joshua just after he finds out he will be repeating third grade. What should they say to him? How can they comfort him? What can they suggest to help him deal with the situation? Have they ever had a similar experience?

4. Have students participate in a panel discussion on the pros and cons of repeating a grade. What benefits are there for the students? Do those benefits outweigh the emotionality of the situation? How should students react?

How should parents react? Perhaps students can come up with some guidelines or suggestions that can be written up in a flyer and distributed through the guidance counselor's office. You might invite the guidance counselor to your class for a series of interviews.

Science/Health

1. Students may be interested in conducting some bird observations. Cut part of the side out of a milk container and fill the bottom with bird seed. Hang the feeder outside your classroom window. Instruct students to observe and record the types of birds that visit the feeder, when they come, how many use it, and the amount of feed consumed. The feeder and records can be maintained for a specific period of time or throughout the school year. A good book on the subject is *A Year of Birds*, by Ashley Wolff (New York: Dodd Mead, 1984).

2. Bring in an old aquarium and have students establish a terrarium that depicts the flora of a particular region of Africa. What kinds of plants, rocks, wood, etc., can be placed in the terrarium so that it accurately represents a region of Africa? Library research may be necessary before beginning this project. If you are interested in obtaining a free catalog of animal containers, including cages, aquariums, terrariums, and birdhouses, write to Martin's Aquarium (101 Old York Road, Route 611, Jenkintown, PA 19046).

3. Invite the school nurse to discuss common childhood injuries, explain how these injuries can be prevented, and how they are treated when they do occur. The nurse may also demonstrate simple first aid procedures.

4. The National Geographic Society (Washington, DC) has a variety of videos that offer students an intriguing look into the richness and vastness of the African continent. Try to obtain one or more of the following: *Africa* (1991 [catalog no. 51440]); *Journey to the Forgotten River* (1990 [catalog no. 51461]); *Serengeti Diary* (1989 [catalog no. 51388]); *African Odyssey* (1988 [catalog no. 51336]); *Bushmen of the Kalahari* (1974 [catalog no. 51027]); *African Wildlife* (catalog no. 50509); *Africa's Stolen River* (1989 [catalog no. 51373]); *Lions of the African Night* (1987 [catalog no. 51331]).

Art

1. Provide students with index cards and ask them to design a postcard that could be sent from Africa to a friend living in the United States. What illustration(s) could be used for the front of the card? Have students collect these postcards and display them on the bulletin board. Some resource books your students will want to consult include *In Africa*, by Marc Bernheim (New York: Atheneum, 1973); *A is for Africa*, by Jean Bond (New York: Watts, 1969); *Wild Animals of Africa*, by Beatrice Borden (New York: Random House, 1982); *Jambo Means Hello*, by Muriel Feelings (New York: Dial Books, 1974); and *Ashanti to Zulu*, by Margaret Musgrove (New York: Dial Books, 1976).

2. Students may enjoy creating a shoebox "jungle." Have students bring in toy animals or create their own out of modeling clay. Trees and bushes can be cut out of construction paper or created out of leaves and twigs found around school. A representation of an African scene can be built inside a shoebox and displayed in the classroom.

Math

1. Demonstrate to students how batting averages are computed (number of hits divided by the number of times at bat). Give them some examples of batting averages from the local newspaper. Have students play one or more games of softball and then compute their individual batting averages (the emphasis is on math, not on who has the highest average!).

2. Involve students in computing their grades for portions of a course or for a selected series of tests or quizzes. You may elect to have students use calculators or a preferred computer program to determine their respective grades. Encourage them to keep track of their grades (show them their scores in your grade book, for example) for a period of time.

3. Have students compute distances from your school to various locations in Africa. Later, they may wish to calculate the travel time to those locations via different vehicles (airplane flying at 450 miles per hour (mph); boat traveling at 12 mph; car going at 50 mph; etc.).

4. Have students construct simple clocks from paper plates and cardboard hands. Ask each to select a city in Africa and determine the time in that city (in comparison with the time in your specific time zone). Occasionally ask students to adjust their clocks to the correct time throughout the day.

Music

1. Students may enjoy listening to true African music. Check with the librarian of your school or local public library for recordings of African music to play for your students. One resource is *African Musical Instruments*, with Bilal Abdurahuram, arranged by Ayyub Addullah (New York: Asch Records). Another is *The Music of Africa Series: Uganda 1* by Hugh Tracey (Washington, DC: Traditional Music Documentation Project, 1972).

2. Contact Folkways Records (New York, NY) and ask for a copy of their current catalog (the school's music teacher or librarian may have a copy). Folkways has an extensive collection of authentic and traditional music from many lands. Obtain one or more recordings to share with your students.

Social Studies

1. Have small groups of students construct travel guides or maps of how Joshua could get to Africa. Have students plan several itineraries and travel routes based on sites to see, cost, or time of year.

2. Students may wish to establish correspondence with a pen pal from Africa. Contact International Pen Pals (P.O. Box 2900065, Brooklyn, NY 11229) and ask for information on sending and receiving letters. Students may also want to correspond with African pen pals through the Afro-Asian Center (P.O. Box 337, Saugerties, NY 12477; 914-246-7828).

3. Have an African food celebration. Bring in a variety of foods native to Africa: honey, dates, coffee, cloves (try clove gum), yams, sunflower seeds, peanuts, grapes, and olives. Have students each write a paragraph describing their reactions to the foods.

Physical Education

1. Ask students to set up and carry out a bicycle rally. What kinds of events would be appropriate (obstacle courses, straight races, closed course for time, etc.)? Students can invent as many different events as possible.

2. Your class may wish to set up a softball tournament with other classes. Decide how many games each team will play and how the tournament victor is to be decided. As part of an art activity, have students design and construct appropriate awards or ribbons for the winners.

THE FOURTH FLOOR TWINS AND THE
FORTUNE COOKIE CHASE
David A. Adler
New York: Puffin Books, 1985

Summary:

Donna and Diane, identical twin sisters, join their fourth-floor neighbors Garry and Kevin to solve the mystery of the "Man in the Blue Hat." The story concerns a fortune-cookie fortune, a mysterious man, coincidence, and suspicion—and it is loaded with adventure.

Critical Thinking Questions:

1. How would the story have been different if Mrs. Lee had put a different fortune in the batch of cookies she gave to the children?

2. Why is it important to the story that there are two sets of twins?

3. What was the significance of the woman and her disguise?

4. Which of the characters in the story did you enjoy most? Which did you enjoy least? State your reasons.

5. If you were writing this story, would you have changed the ending? Why or why not?

Reading/Language Arts

1. Ask students to make a master list of the occupations they would like to enter when they grow up. Have students prepare sets of questions they would like to ask individuals in those occupations. Send teams of students into the local community to interview people in the selected occupations and bring responses back to the class for sharing and discussion, Later, students can combine their information into a newsletter or series of occupational brochures.

2. Have students write letters to friends about what they enjoyed most about the book. What characters or events were most enjoyable? What kinds of changes would they suggest the author make in the book if it were to be written again?

3. Have a small group of students put together a sequel to the book in the form of a play or skit. What other kinds of adventures would the twins have? Afterward, students may enjoy reading another book in the Fourth Floor Twins series, *The Fourth Floor Twins and the Disappearing Parrot Trick*, by David A. Adler (New York: Viking, 1986).

4. Ask students to pretend to be neighbors of the twins. Ask them to write about what they observe the twins doing and the reasons why the twins take those actions. How do students feel about living on the same floor as the twins? What is different about that living situation and their own living situations?

5. Have students prepare horoscopes for Donna, Diane, Garry, and Kevin. Show them examples from the local newspaper and ask them to create some original horoscopes for the four major characters with particular reference to events that take place in the story. These can then be posted in the classroom.

Science/Health

1. Have students take a survey of other students in the school to determine the various kinds of pets students have. How many different varieties are there? Instruct students to compile a master list organized by the primary families of animals (mammals, fish, amphibians, birds, reptiles). Have students discuss reasons why one family of animal seems to be more popular as pets than others.

2. Obtain a copy of the National Geographic Society filmstrip series entitled *Animals, Animals* (Washington, DC: 1990 [catalog no. 30619]). These two sound filmstrips describe how animals are classified and why some animals live in groups. Discuss with students how their pets at home fit into the topics discussed in these filmstrips.

3. Check with a local veterinarian and obtain or borrow a chart of dog or cat diseases. What kinds of diseases usually plague these two popular pets? How can the health of dogs and cats be maintained? If possible, invite a vet to visit the class and discuss pet diseases and disease prevention.

Art

1. Have one group of students create posters for lost pets (they may choose to use their own pets as the lost ones). Another group of students can create some classified advertisements for lost or missing pets. Have students discuss which approach would be most effective in locating a missing animal.

2. Challenge students to create a disguise (head and face) that would allow them to pass unnoticed through the school. What kinds of art materials, clothing, supplies, and procedures could be combined to create an effective disguise? Students may wish to work together in groups to create a single disguise for one individual.

3. Provide students with paper lunch bags and ask them to create their own verions of the blue hat. Using poster paints, scissors, and glue, have students invent a replica of the blue hat. Then, in a retelling of the story, one student can be chosen as the man in the blue hat to act out specific scenes.

Math

1. Have students create their own word problems with fortune cookies. Obtain a large supply of fortune cookies from a local supermarket or oriental restaurant. Have students invent word problems using those cookies. For example, if each of the twins had seven fortune cookies and Diane ate three of them, how many fortune cookies would be left? Students can create their own problems to share with each other (this process becomes easier when students can manipulate actual objects such as the fortune cookies).

Music

1. Play Saint-Saëns's *Carnival of the Animals* for students. Ask them to discuss the various instruments used and how each instrument is made to sound like a particular animal. What instruments do they have or can they create to imitate the sounds of various animals? Examples of various instruments students can make themselves can be found in *Make Mine Music*, by Tom Walther (Boston: Little, Brown, 1981).

Social Studies

1. Set up a career corner in the classroom. Have students send away for brochures and information packets from various organizations. (Your school or public librarians can provide you with addresses for the occupations students are most interested in.) As the information arrives, have students assemble it into attractive displays. You may elect to work with a colleague and have two classes cooperate on this project.

2. Divide the class into several groups and challenge each group to draw a map of the school or a section of the school. Later, have students compare their maps and discuss the need for accuracy in maps. What might be the consequences if maps were not accurate? How would the twins or the policeman have benefited from using a map to locate the barn in the story?

Physical Education

1. Students can play a game of "Hide and Seek." After one round of the game, ask students to create modifications of the game. For example, two students could hide in different locations, the object being to find both of them within a specified time period. Or the game can be organized on a team basis, with an entire team hiding from the other. Encourage students to develop as many different variations as possible.

2. Have students play a game of "Twin Tag." Two students hook arms and chase after other students without letting go of each other. When another student is tagged, he or she remains "frozen" until touched by another student.

M & M AND THE MUMMY MESS
Pat Ross
New York: Viking Penguin, 1985

Summary:

At the natural history museum, Mandy and Mimi took a sneak preview of the Mummy Wonders exhibit. After being discovered by the museum director, they are used as part of the advertisement for the tour. One of a series of M & M books.

Critical Thinking Questions:

1. What is most interesting about visiting a museum? What is the most interesting thing you have seen at a museum?

2. What would you enjoy most about being an archaeologist? What would you enjoy least?

3. Why do you think M & M sneaked into the closed display area? Have you ever done anything like that?

4. Where do you like to go with your friends? Are there any possible adventures at any of those places? Which place has the most possibilities for an adventure?

Reading/Language Arts

1. Challenge students to write a new ending to the book, starting at the point when the museum director found Mandy and Mimi in the tour that was temporarily closed.

2. Have students make up a master list of all the things they would like to be buried with if they were one of the ancient Egyptians. How similar are the lists between individual students? Can the class agree on one or two items that everyone would like to have with them? Ask students to defend, in writing or orally, their reasons for choosing the items they did.

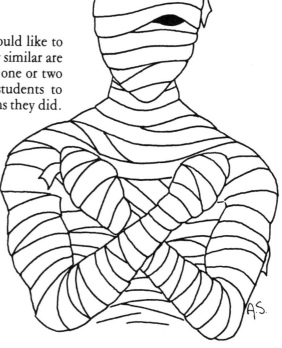

3. Have students try to invent their own recipe on how to wrap a mummy (students may wish to experiment with papier-mâché or a mixture of flour and water). The resultant recipes should be written up so that others may copy them. Old rag dolls or well-used stuffed animals can serve as surrogate mummies. Students may enjoy reading the book *Mummies Made in Egypt*, by Aliki (New York: Crowell, 1979).

4. "Strange" poetry can be shared with students on a daily basis. Several examples can be obtained from the book *Creatures* by Lee Bennett Hopkins (San Diego: Harcourt Brace Jovanovich, 1985).

5. Have students compose a biography entitled "A Day in the Life of a Mummy." Encourage them to be inventive in describing the events and actions of their mummy during the course of one twenty-four-hour period.

6. Students will enjoy reading other M & M books, including: *M & M and the Bad News Babies*, by Pat Ross (New York: Puffin Books, 1983); *M & M and the Haunted House Game*, by Pat Ross (New York: Pantheon, 1980); *M & M and the Big Bag*, by Pat Ross (New York: Pantheon, 1981); and *Meet M & M*, by Pat Ross (New York: Pantheon, 1980).

Science/Health

1. Survey students to determine who has ever had a broken bone. Invite a local doctor to visit the class to explain what a cast is as well as its purposes. Ask the doctor to bring a sample cast (or perhaps some casting materials) to demonstrate.

2. Students can investigate the processes involved in decay through several simple experiments. For example, bring in several pieces of food (fruit or meat) and place some of the samples on the windowsill in open containers. Place other samples in sealed bags in a refrigerator. Ask students to observe the various samples over a period of several days and record their observations. To what do they attribute the differences between the various samples? How does this experiment relate to the mummification process practiced by the ancient Egyptians?

3. An excellent video, which can be obtained from the National Geographic Society (Washington, DC 20036), is *Egypt's Pyramids: Houses of Eternity* (1978 [catalog no. 51056]). Although the film is intended for older students, it provides valuable information and a forum for much discussion on the burial habits of the ancient Egyptians.

Art

1. Provide students with pipe cleaners and ask them to create models of people or animals. Afterward, have students wrap their models with tissue paper (to resemble mummies) and place them in a diorama of an ancient Egyptian site.

2. Ask students to create their own posters to advertise the Mummy Wonders tour at a fictitious museum of natural history. What features or exhibits should be included on the posters to entice people to visit the museum?

Math

1. Call a local museum and obtain the admission prices for various people (adults, students, children under the age of six, servicepersons, senior citizens, etc.). Have students create their own math problems by calculating the total cost for taking the entire class, their families, four families from their neighborhoods, or any other arrangement to the museum.

2. Have students take each other's measurements (height and width). Ask them to determine what types of sarcophagi (large, medium, small) they would need to accommodate the different measurements. Have students design appropriate sarcophagi using their own measurements.

Music

1. Students may be interested in trying to construct some ancient musical instruments such as the lyre, lute, and aeolian harp. Directions can be found in *Make Mine Music*, by Tom Walther (Boston: Little, Brown, 1981).

Social Studies

1. Show the class the filmstrip series Ancient Civilizations (Washington, DC: National Geographic Society, 1978 [catalog no. 03972]), a series of five sound filmstrips including one entitled *Mesopotamia and Egypt.* Have the class discuss the contributions ancient Egyptians made to civilizations in general and modern life today.

2. Check with a local college to find out if there is an egyptologist (or expert on ancient civilizations) willing to make a presentation to your class (a museum curator might also be a potential speaker). If possible, have the visitor bring in artifacts from the time period under discussion to show students. Afterward, have students make up their own guidebook to the customs and traditions of that time period.

3. Have students construct a salt-dough map of Egypt. (Mix one part flour with one-half part salt. Slowly add one-third part water and squeeze the mixture until it is smooth.) The map can be crafted on a large piece of cardborad or plywood and painted with tempera paint when dry. Have students locate and identify major landforms, cities, and other geographical features.

4. Contact a local travel agent for brochures and other descriptive information on travel to and in Egypt. Have students set up a display on sites and attractions to see when visiting Egypt.

Physical Education

1. Conduct a series of "Mummy Races." Have two students stand next to each other and wrap their adjoining legs with an Ace bandage or gauze. Teams of students then race to a designated finishing point. Two students can have their opposite arms wrapped with gauze for another kind of race. Two students can stand back to back with their thighs wrapped together for an even more difficult race.

2. In the book, the two girls sneaked under the ropes of the closed tour. Have students practice different ways of going under a progressively lowered rope (crawling, limbo, etc.).

NEW NEIGHBORS FOR NORA
Johanna Hurwitz
New York: Morrow, 1979

Summary:

Nora is a precocious seven-year-old who lives in a New York City apartment building. The story focuses on Nora's neighbors, both young and old. Nora tells about who she likes in her building, who she dislikes, and what she thinks about her new neighbors.

Critical Thinking Questions:

1. If you could be neighbors with anyone in the world, who would you choose? If you could have any five people as neighbors, who would they be?

2. If you could be any character in this story, which one would you choose? Why?

3. When was the last time you lied about something? How do you feel when you get caught? Why do you think people sometimes lie?

4. What would you enjoy most about staying home from school for a long period of time? What would you like least?

5. What are some of your favorite names for a baby boy? For a baby girl? What is it about those names that you like most?

Reading/Language Arts

1. Have students create a collage about their friends and neighbors. They can paste photographs or pictures cut from old magazines onto pieces of construction paper. When completed, have children given oral presentations of their collages to the rest of the class.

2. Have children design an award that they would want to give to a favorite neighbor or friend. These can be designed on construction paper and awarded at an awards ceremony. Encourage students to prepare speeches they would use at an actual ceremony.

3. Direct each student to write a letter of appreciation to the author telling her why they enjoyed the book. These letters can be sent to the author in care of the publisher (William Morrow & Co., 105 Madison Avenue, New York, NY 10016). Your students may get a response from the author.

4. Other books by Johanna Hurwitz that the students will enjoy reading include: *Class Clown* (New York: Morrow, 1987); *Much Ado About Aldo* (New York: Morrow, 1978); *Russell Rides Again* (New York: Morrow, 1985); and *Super Duper Teddy* (New York: Morrow, 1980).

Science/Health

1. Have students study rain and its effects. They may wish to set up a special rain station to record the amount of rain that falls in a given period of time. An inexpensive weather station that indicates wind direction, wind speed, rainfall, and temperature can be obtained through Nasco (901 Janesville Avenue, Fort Atkinson, WI 53538; 800-558-9595). The acidity of the rain can be measured with litmus paper (obtained from your local high school). The effects of rain in terms of erosion can be calculated at an outdoor site on the school grounds. Students will also enjoy other books about rain, such as *Bringing the Rain to Kapiti Plain*, by Verna Aardema (New York: Dial Books, 1985) and *Rain and Hail*, by Franklyn Branley (New York: Crowell, 1983).

2. Invite the school nurse to visit the class and give a talk on dental health. The nurse can talk about foods that are good for the teeth as well as those that might be harmful. Ask the nurse to provide students with instruction on brushing their teeth properly, too.

3. Students may be interested in investigating various childhood diseases such as chicken pox. How are they contracted, prevented, and treated? A comparative chart may be constructed listing the information gathered. A local pediatrician could visit the class to add additional information. Students may be interested in reading *Peter Gets the Chickenpox*, by Marguerite Lerner (New York: Lerner, 1959) and *Betsy and the Chicken Pox*, by Gunilla Wolde (New York: Random House, 1976).

4. Students may enjoy creating a small classroom garden filled with plants such as beans and radishes. "Crystallite Indoor Greenhouse" can be obtained through Nasco (see address in activity 1). Ask students to record the growth of the plants over a period of time and chart the changes that occur. Miniature gardens can be prepared in shoeboxes and kept outside or indoors under ultraviolet lights.

Art

1. Have children design a series of get-well cards. These can be illustrated and written using examples from a local card shop. When a student becomes sick, one of the cards can be selected, signed by all members of the class, and sent to the ill student.

2. Have children make sketches comparing the changes in the clothing styles over the last twenty years or so. What kinds of clothes did children wear during the time this story took place? What kinds of clothes do children wear today? Students may wish to make a two-sided poster illustrating the differences.

3. Students may enjoy making papier-mâché heads of several of the characters in the book. The heads can be constructed life-sized or in smaller proportions and displayed along a windowsill or shelf in the room.

Math

1. Ask students to predict the length of time this story took. Have each one construct a time line that lists or illustrates important events from the story, when each event occurred, and the approximate time each one took. Ask students to compare and discuss their different time lines.

2. Have students discuss the changes that babies go through during their early years of development (you may wish to discuss the growth and development of your own children or those of a friend or neighbor). Have students create baby calendars that list the developmental stages of babies and the approximate times these events take place. Some interesting resources for students include: *101 Things to Do with a Baby*, by Jan Ormerod (New York: Lothrop, 1984), *Being Born*, by Sheila Kitzinger (New York: Grosset, 1986), or the students' own baby books.

3. Children can guess how many steps Nora and her friends had to run up and down in their apartment building. They can compare their guesses with the number of stairs in several apartment buildings in your community. Have students chart the number of steps or stairwells in an apartment building. Is there an average number of steps in a flight of stairs? In an entire stairwell? In different apartment buildings?

Music

1. Have students make up a get-well song using the music from a popular song and their own invented lyrics. The final song can be sung and recorded on cassette tape. When a student is sick, the tape can be sent home to be played and enjoyed. Be sure to leave space at the end of the tape for students to record personal messages and greetings to the sick classmate.

2. Have students sing the song, "Rain, Rain, Go Away." Ask them to construct raindrops in the form of musical notes, each of which can be placed on an oversized bar scale representing the song.

Social Studies

1. Provide each of several small groups of students with a single uncooked egg. Direct each group to decide how the egg will be cared for over the next twenty-four hours so that it does not crack, making sure that everyone has a chance to carry it around during part of the day.

2. Have students discuss the different types of housing people live in. Construct a large mural illustrating the various forms of houses used in this country as well as the different dwellings used in other countries. Which ones seem to be most comfortable? Which ones are most portable? Which ones are specifically designed for the local environment and could not be used in other locations?

3. Students may wish to correspond with the residents of a local nursing home (be sure to get permission first). Each child (or small group of students) can "adopt" a resident of the nursing home as a foster grandparent. Lines of communication can be established and occasional visits can be scheduled throughout the year.

4. Have students go through the Yellow Pages of the phone book and make a list of the various services that would be needed by people in an apartment building. What kinds of services would apartment dwellers need that would not be necessary for single-family homes?

Physical Education

1. Have students devise and participate in their own "Rainy Day Decathlon." Cotton balls can be used as shotputs and thrown for distance. Paper plates can substitute for discuses and be thrown for distance. Straws can substitute

for javelins. Encourage students to create their own events based on those in the Olympics and keep these events handy for the occasional rainy day.

2. Have students devise an indoor fitness program. What types of exercises can be done indoors to maintain physical fitness?

SOMETHING QUEER AT THE HAUNTED SCHOOL
Elizabeth Levy
New York: Dell Publishing, 1982

Summary:

Just days before Halloween, something queer begins to happen at Jill and Gwen's school. Some believe a werewolf is the cause of the deafening screams and spooky noises, but Jill and Gwen have other ideas. The unraveling of this mystery is filled with excitement, adventure, and plenty of haunting.

Critical Thinking Questions:

1. What could have happened if Mr. Murdoch had not been caught?

2. What do you think was the most important clue that Jill and Gwen discovered when solving the mystery?

3. What would you do if you were the principal? Would you fire Mr. Murdoch or let him teach? Why?

4. Would you have been as brave as Jill and Gwen in solving the case? What would you have done differently?

5. What strange things have taken place at your school? How were these mysteries solved?

Reading/Language Arts

1. Ask a group of students to create an original ghost story. One student begins the story with an opening paragraph. Another student adds a paragraph to the first one. Another student adds another paragraph, and so on. It would be appropriate to tape record the invented story and play it back for students. They may decide to make alterations or adjustments in the story before presenting it, in written or oral form, to classmates.

2. Have students retell the story, emphasizing the steps Jill and Gwen took to ultimately unravel the mystery. Students should then be encouraged to create their own book entitled *How to Solve Mysteries*, a compendium of tips from the book as well as ideas from class members, friends, and relatives. The final book can be submitted to the school library for cataloging.

3. Ask students to select a portion of the book and develop it into a radio play. Character voices, special sound effects, and a narrator can all be combined into a short skit that can be played over the school's intercom system.

4. Students will enjoy reading other mystery stories, particularly those in a series. Series such as the Cam Jansen series by David Adler and the Encyclopedia Brown series by Donald Sobol are particularly appropriate.

5. Other books by the same author that your students will enjoy include: *Frankenstein Moved in on the Fourth Floor* (New York: Harper and Row, 1979); *The Shadow Nose* (New York: Morrow, 1983); and *Something Queer Is Going On* (New York: Dell Publishing, 1973).

Science/Health

1. Post an oversized calendar for the month in the front of the classroom. Ask students to look at the moon each evening (when possible) and draw a diagram of it for transfer to the classroom calendar. Discuss with students the phases the moon goes through during the month and what each phase signifies. Students may be interested in the following resources: *Moongame*, by Frank Asch (New York: Prentice-Hall, 1984) and *The Moon Seems to Change*, by Franklyn Branley (New York: Crowell, 1987).

2. Just for fun, have students create a werewolf's menu. Students should make decisions about the types of food this type of animal might enjoy. Also, students should consider a werewolf's possible habitat and concentrate on the types of food and prey found in this area. Should a werewolf eat foods from all four food groups to stay healthy?

3. Students may wish to assemble a scrapbook of facts, figures, myths, and mysteries about wolves. They should check with the school or local librarian for related books. Two to start with include *The First Dog*, by Jan Brett (San Diego, CA: Harcourt, 1988) and *A First Look at Dogs*, by Millicent Selsam (New York: Walker, 1981).

Art

1. Bring in some squash (or pumpkins, if available) and instruct students on the proper procedures for carving jack-o'-lanterns. Ask students to draw illustrations on how several jack-o'-lanterns could be carved (with you doing the actual carving). Each lantern can be embellished with scraps of fabric, lace, yarn, buttons, and other items.

2. Ask several students to lie down on a large sheet of newsprint. Trace the outlines of these students and cut the silhouettes out. Provide small groups of students with one of the outlines and challenge them to create an original werewolf (provide them with pictures, if necessary). Afterward, post the werewolves in the classroom.

3. If possible, obtain a large appliance box from a local store and ask students to turn it into a miniature haunted house. Students can paint scenes, objects, and designs that would be associated with a haunted house on the outside of the box. When the whole house has been painted, a small window can be cut in the side so that a student seated inside the box can read portions of the book to classmates.

Math

1. Invite a seamstress or tailor to your classroom to discuss how measurements are taken for clothing (individual students can serve as models). Ask students to use that information to take measurements of all the students in the classroom. A large chart can be posted with that information recorded.

2. Ask students to conduct a poll of favorite or popular monsters. Students can develop a questionnaire to be given in person or in writing to other students throughout the school. Students may wish to compare the monster preferences of boys versus girls or among different grade levels. The results should be tallied and recorded in the form of bar graphs or percentages.

3. Sound travels at about 738 mph. Ask students to determine how far sound would travel in ten minutes; in one-half hour; in sixty seconds. Work with students to estimate how far away the werewolf was when Jill and Gwen heard it howl.

Music

1. Ask students to create a variety of sound effects that could be used along with a reading of the book. What musical instruments would create sounds of a werewolf, a haunted house, a creep night, etc.? Can students use common household objects (bottles, spoons, newspapers) to create appropriate sound effects?

Social Studies

1. Students will be interested in learning about some of the customs surrounding Halloween. Provide them with data from one or more of the following books: *Let's Find Out About Halloween*, Paulette Cooper (New York: Watts, 1972); *Halloween*, by Gail Gibbons (New York: Holiday, 1984); or *Halloween*, by Helen Borten (New York: Crowell, 1965).

2. Discuss with students the factors or events that might lead to a house becoming haunted. What social, economic, or historical events might contribute to the eventual haunting of a particular house? Later, students may enjoy putting together a guide entitled "How to Turn Your House into a Haunted House."

Physical Education

1. Ask students to put together a physical fitness guide for monsters. What kinds of exercise should specific monsters do in order to stay in shape? Invite the physical education teacher to discuss exercises appropriate for different body types (since monsters come in all sizes) as well as those appropriate for students.

2. Invite students to create a "monster dance" using a popular song. What new steps or movements can they invent that would be appropriate for selected monsters to use? Students may wish to work individually or in small groups.

THAT MUSHY STUFF
Judy Delton
New York: Dell Publishing, 1989

Summary:

Molly Duff and the other Pee Wee Scouts have adventures while earning merit badges and doing good deeds. At the same time, they must occasionally struggle with childhood relationships and problems. One of a series of books about the Pee Wee Scouts.

Critical Thinking Questions:

1. What are some things you and your classmates could do to help out in your local community?

2. Why do people tease each other? How do you feel when you get teased? How does it feel to be the teaser?

3. How old do you think children should be before they have a boyfriend or girlfriend? Why?

4. What would you enjoy most about being a member of a group of scouts? What kinds of activities would you like to participate in?

5. What would you enjoy most about working in a hospital? What would you enjoy least? What types of challenges do hospital workers face on their jobs?

Reading/Language Arts

1. Ask students to write a paragraph in their journals about a deed or deeds they have done that made them feel particularly good about themselves. Encourage students to share their paragraphs orally, if they choose.

2. Ask students to make up a time chart of the six most important events in the story. These can be listed in writing or as illustrations. The time line should be posted in the classroom.

3. Encourage students to read other books in the Pee Wee Scouts series. Ask them to share and discuss the book they enjoyed the most. Which did they like the least? What qualities made one book more enjoyable than another? Students may also enjoy reading other books by the same author, including *Two Good Friends* (New York: Crown, 1974) and *A Birthday Bike for Brimhall* (Minneapolis, MN: Carolrhoda, 1985).

4. Divide the class into groups. Have students invent and write short stories on the possible origin of St. Valentine's Day. Ask groups to share their creations with each other.

Science/Health

1. Contact your local chapter of the American Red Cross and invite a representative to visit your classroom to demonstrate proper first aid techniques. If possible, ask the representative to bring the CPR dummy to demonstrate.

2. Students may devise their own solar cookers. Have them punch a hole in either end of a shoebox and line the shoebox with aluminum foil, shiny side up. A skewer can be placed through one hole, through a hot dog, and through the hole in the other side of the box. The box should be placed outside in the sun. Have students check the hot dog every half hour or so for doneness. If you wish, you can obtain a "Portable Solar Cooker" from Edmund Scientific (101 East Glouchester Pike, Barrington, NJ 08007; 800-257-6173).

3. Invite a representative of the American Lung Association to make a presentation to the class on the dangers of smoking. Afterward, have students design brochures about the effects of smoking on the lungs.

Art

1. Have students prepare anti-smoking posters to be hung around the community. Challenge students to invent a series of anti-smoking slogans to be included along with the posters.

2. Invite students to create a wordless picture book using important events from the story. This activity can be done in small groups with each group displaying its book on the bulletin board.

3. Provide students with the necessary art materials and ask them to create Valentine cards to send to their parents. It does not have to be Valentine's Day for this activity—students can create and send their cards any time.

Math

1. Have students conduct a school survey to find out how many students in the school belong to various scouting groups (Cub Scouts, Boy Scouts, Girl Scouts, Blue Birds, Camp Fire Girls, etc.). Afterward, have students figure the percentage of students belonging to each group (in comparison with the entire school population or the number of students at a particular grade level). Students may use pie charts or bar graphs to record their data.

2. Have students visit a local grocery store or drugstore to price a selected list of items in a first aid kit (bandages, ointments, tape, scissors, etc.). Have them add up the cost of assembling a homemade first aid kit and compare that price with the price(s) of ready-made kits.

3. Have students research the price of a pack of cigarettes. Challenge them to compute the costs involved if a person smoked a pack a day: how much would it cost per week; per month; per year? What if a person smoked a pack and a half or two packs a day? Afterward, have students make a list of alternate ways of spending those amounts of money.

Music

1. Check with the school's music teacher and put together a song book of favorite camp songs. Share some of these songs with students (for example, "She'll Be Comin' Round the Mountain" and "The Ghost of John").

2. Encourage students to sing the Pee Wee Scout song in the back of the book to the tune of "Old MacDonald Had a Farm."

Social Studies

1. Invite local scout leaders to visit your classroom and talk about the opportunities available through their respective programs. If possible, have the visitors explain the history of their groups and the contributions made by group members to the local community.

2. Brainstorm with the students to create a list of good deeds that could be done for other students or for the school (set up a tutoring center, read to younger students, clean up litter on the playground). Ask students to put one of their suggestions into action.

3. If possible, set up a campground on the school grounds. Have students bring in tents, sleeping bags, and other camping equipment to be used for a day. Move your classroom to the campground for the day and conduct all your lessons there. Afterward, have students discuss some of the advantages or difficulties encountered.

Physical Education

1. Invite a local expert to your class to explain orienteering (contact a local hiking club or scouting group). Ask the visitor to take the class through a demonstration of orienteering on the school grounds.

2. Invite students to create an outdoor obstacle course of physical activities such as crawling under a rope, stepping through tires, climbing over the jungle gym, etc.

GRADE 4

■ ━━ ■

CATWINGS RETURN
Ursula K. LeGuin
New York: Orchard Books, 1989

Summary:

Four winged cats living in the country remember their mother and their home in a city dumpster. Two of the winged cats decide to return and visit their mother. They find the city different and discover a frightened winged kitten in a deserted warehouse that is being demolished. The three leave and find their mother, but decide to leave her to return to the country.

Critical Thinking Questions:

1. What would you do if you found a catwing?

2. How do you think the animals felt about leaving their mother? Have you ever experienced anything similar to that? Can you describe your feelings at the time?

3. What would you name the new kitten? Why would you choose that particular name?

4. If the catwings were your pets, where would you keep them? Would you want to show them to your friends? Your parents? Your classmates?

5. Have you ever felt frightened and alone? Describe a single situation when you felt frightened. How was the situation resolved?

Reading/Language Arts

1. Before reading the book, show the picture of the winged cats from the book. Divide the class into small groups. Direct one student in each group to write a sentence about what he or she thinks the story will be about. The second student in each group continues by adding his or her own ideas. The predicted story continues with each student adding an idea or two. When completed, have a representative from each group read the predicted story to the rest of the class.

2. Students will enjoy reading other books by the same author. Some possibilities include: *Catwings* (New York: Watts, 1988); *Solomon Leviathan's Nine Hundred and Thirty-First Trip Around the World* (New York: Putnam, 1988); *A Visit from Dr. Katz* (New York: Atheneum, 1988); and *A Wizard of Earthsea* (New York: Atheneum, 1971).

3. Have students make predictions about different ways that cats could fly. Then have them read *Cat and the Canary*, by Michael Foreman (New York: Dial Books, 1985) about a cat who flies with the aid of a kite.

Science/Health

1. Invite a local veterinarian to your class to discuss cats. The vet should be able to explain the various types of cats, their eating and sleeping habits, and their care and well-being. If possible, have the vet bring brochures and other appropriate literature to be included in a bulletin board display.

2. Students may want to make bird feeders to hang outside a classroom window. Cut a section from the side of a milk carton and fill with birdseed. Hang the feeder in a tree or other convenient location. Another type of feeder can be made by taking refrigerated bread stick dough (Pillsbury makes one variety) and rolling it in birdseed. The dough can be formed into a circle, dried or baked and hung with string on a tree branch. Make sure students keep accurate records of the varieties of birds that use their feeders.

3. Have students check the books in the school library or public library about cats (there are literally hundreds of fiction books available). Have students combine their library research into a cat scrapbook, called *All about Cats*, that also includes information and photographs of students' pet cats.

Art

1. Have students create some "Combo Creatures." Provide students with copies of old magazines. Your librarian may have discards. Have them cut out different animal parts and paste them together to create new creatures. Students may wish to act out how each of the Combo Creatures might act, behave, or sound.

2. Have students cut out pictures of various types of cats from several nature magazines. Turn each picture over and brush on a mixture of one tablespoon of honey and one tablespoon of water. Let them dry and dust with cornstarch. These stickers can then be licked and placed on homework papers or other appropriate places.

3. Have students create oversized wings for themselves out of butcher paper. Paint the wings in bright colors and mount them on the walls of the classroom (as part of a language arts activity, direct students to imagine that they can fly with those wings and to write or tell of an adventure they had while using their own wings).

Math

1. Have students measure each other's "wingspan." Each child holds his or her arms out to the side and a measurement is taken from fingertip to fingertip. These measurements can be combined into categories and recorded in the form of a graph or chart.

2. Have students conduct some library research to locate the physical dimensions (height, weight, length, etc.) of various members of the cat family (tigers, lion, ocelots, lynx, etc.). Direct students to prepare charts of the accumulated data.

Music

1. Have students invent their own cat songs using the music from another song. For example, here is a song that can be sung to the tune of "Old MacDonald Had a Farm":
   Hank and Susan found some cats, ee-eye, ee-eye, oh!
   And oh, those cats, how they could fly, ee-eye, ee-eye, oh!
   With a whoosh, whoosh here
   And a flap, flap there
   Here a whoosh, there a flap, everywhere a whoosh, whoosh
   Hank and Susan found some cats, ee-eye, ee-eye, oh!

Social Studies

1. Make a tape recording of city sounds and a tape recording of country sounds (have colleagues, friends, or relatives in other parts of the country help you). Have students listen to both and discuss or write what sounds, sights, and smells would be found in both locations.

2. Invite a speaker from the local chapter of the ASPCA or Humane Society to discuss unwanted pets and what is done about them.

3. The National Geographic Society (Washington, DC) produces a fascinating series of six sound filmstrips in their Our World series. Part Two (1989 [catalog no. 30506]) deals with *Neighborhoods* and *Communities* and would be an excellent supplement to the book.

4. Students may be interested in learning more about the demolition of buildings. Check your local Yellow Pages for the names of demolition contractors. Contact one and invite a representative to visit your classroom to explain the procedures and safety precautions that must be taken when demolishing a building. Students should be prepared to ask questions.

Physical Education

1. Schedule an "Animal Walk Relay." Have the class assemble into two teams. A list of animals is posted on the chalkboard. The first member of each team must imitate the walk of the first animal. The second member of each team must imitate the walk of the second animal, and so on (practice sessions may be needed beforehand). The first team to complete the list is the winner. Examples of some potential animals include: cat, kangaroo, gorilla, dog.

CHOCOLATE FEVER
Robert Kimmel Smith
New York: Dell Yearling, 1972

Summary:

Henry Green is a typical boy, except that he loves chocolate to excess. One day, Henry starts breaking out in brown spots, each with the aroma of chocolate. Frightened by all the attention he gets, Henry runs away, only to get himself into more trouble. By the end of this tale, Henry learns about friendship and about some important lessons in life.

Critical Thinking Questions:

1. What would you have done if you had noticed brown spots on yourself? Would you react in the same manner as Henry did?

2. After Henry runs away from the hospital, he begins to "think out his situation." What does this mean?

3. What qualities do you enjoy most about your friends? How do people become friends?

4. Running away from a situation is rarely an answer. What do you think Henry should have done?

5. Henry was lucky to have been picked up by Mac. However, what kinds of dangers does hitchhiking present, particularly to young people?

Reading/Language Arts

1. Provide students with books about chocolate and the chocolate industry. Here's one to get you started: *Cocoa Beans and Daisies*, by Pascale Allamand (New York: Warne, 1978). Students may also wish to write to chocolate manufacturers to ask for informational literature and brochures on the manufacture of chocolate. When students have collected a sufficient amount of data, ask them to create their own guide to chocolate, including where it is grown and how it is harvested, shipped, handled, processed, and manufactured.

2. Ask each student to bring a favorite chocolate recipe from home. These may range from complex recipes for eclairs and petit fours to more simple recipes for brownies and fudge. Encourage students to include the widest variety of recipes possible. Each of these recipes can be transcribed onto sheets of paper and collected into a classroom recipe book for display in the library (of course, you will want to prepare one or more of the recipes in the classroom, too).

3. Ask a small group of students to create a skit about a hospital emergency room. Students may wish to visit the emergency room of a local hospital to get a sense of the events that take place there. Later, they can combine their observations into a short presentation for other members of the class.

Science/Health

1. Arrange to have a doctor, a nurse, and a paramedic visit your classroom for a panel discussion on hospital procedures and emergency room care. What types of patients are typically seen in emergency rooms? What are some of the more unusual cases? What kind of training is necessary for work in an emergency room? What is the relationship among paramedics, nurses, and doctors?

2. Have students develop their own experiments using chocolate syrup. For example, what happens when chocolate syrup is poured into containers of water, milk, salad oil, orange juice, vinegar, or other liquids? Does it sink to the bottom or float on top? What reasons can students offer for these differences and what can they infer about the properties of chocolate syrup?

3. Students will enjoy conducting some kitchen experiments with chocolate. They should obtain copies of one of the following books and note the chocolate-related demonstrations: *Messing Around with Baking Chemistry*, by Bernie Zubrowski (Boston: Little, Brown, 1981) and *Kitchen Chemistry: Science Experiments to Do at Home*, by Robert Gardner (New York: Messner, 1982).

Art

1. Have students create posters on the dangers of hitchhiking. The finished posters can be hung in the classroom or throughout the school. You may wish to invite a local police officer to your classroom to give students the necessary background information on hitchhiking before the posters are designed.

2. Obtain a refrigerator box from a local appliance store and challenge students to create a replica of the cabin in the book. Because the story does not provide much description of the cabin, students will feel free to use their imaginations concerning style, colors, and layout of their cabin.

Math

1. Challenge students to increase or decrease the measurements for a chocolate recipe according to the number of people who will be eating it. For example, a recipe for a single chocolate ice cream soda is:

   3 tablespoons chocolate syrup
   2 scoops vanilla ice cream
   6 ounces chilled club soda

   Have students increase the recipe for a party of fourteen people, a party of five people, and a party of twenty-two people.

2. Have students calculate the number of servings or the amounts that can be obtained from one or more chocolate recipes. For example, if brownies are baked in a 13-by-9-inch pan and there are 20 students in the class, what size will each piece be if everyone gets an equal-sized piece?

Music

1. Challenge students to put together a collection of songs that use "candy words" in their titles or as part of the lyrics. Can they collect old songs as well as popular songs that are "sweet" or "sugar coated"? Do any songs use "chocolate" words in the title or lyrics?

Social Studies

1. The book mentions the names of two explorers, Marco Polo and Amerigo Vespucci. Divide the class in half and direct each group to research the life and times of one of these two explorers. What did they contribute to our knowledge of the world? Why are they considered famous explorers? How do we honor their exploits?

2. Have students investigate various types of communities in the United States. What is meant by an urban community? A suburban one? A rural one? What type of community do most of the students live in? Have small groups of students each develop a handbook on life in one of the three major types of communities (urban, suburban, rural). What type of information should be included in each guide?

3. Mac said that he was used to the way people stared at him because of his skin color. Have students discuss the nature and causes of racial discrimination. Why do people discriminate against one another solely because of skin color? How should society deal with racial discrimination? How would students feel if they were considered less than adequate simply because of skin color?

4. Since a great deal of our chocolate and cocoa beans come from South America, students may be interested in a National Geographic Society (Washington, DC) video entitled *South America* (1991 [catalog no. 51441]).

Physical Education

1. Students may enjoy creating different kinds of relay races, each of which uses a piece of chocolate candy as the "baton." For example, groups of students can line up on opposite sides of a room, run towards each other, exchange several candy bars, and run back to their teammates. Two more members of the team do the same thing until everyone has completed the "run and exchange." The team finishing first is the winner.

CLASS CLOWN
Johanna Hurwitz
New York: Morrow, 1987

Summary:

Lucas is one of the smartest children in his class. However, he is very rambunctious and always ends up being the class clown. Nevertheless, Lucas shows everyone and himself that he is really intelligent when he replaces the ringmaster in a school play at the last minute. Lucas learns that there is a time and a place for everything, including humor.

Critical Thinking Questions:

1. If your teacher sent an unsealed note home to your parents with you, would you be tempted to read it? If it contained bad news, would you still share it with your parents? Why?

2. If you could play any part in a circus, which part would you choose and why?

3. Have you ever known anyone like Lucas, that is, a class clown? How do students react to a class clown? How do adults?

4. Would you be able to go for an entire day without talking to anyone? What would you need to do to accomplish this feat?

5. What part(s) in a play do you enjoy most? Playing a major role? A minor role? Being behind the scenes?

Reading/Language Arts

1. Have students pretend that they are teachers. Ask each one to compose a note to send home to the parents of a child who is misbehaving in class. What kinds of things would they tell the parents? What would they suggest the parents do?

2. Ask students to prepare two different summaries of the book. Present one summary as though the student were a class clown (a humorous rendition). Present the other version as if the student were a class bully (a boisterous presentation). Ask other students to relate what they liked or disliked about each telling.

3. Have students make journal entries on what they would need to do in order to "turn over a new leaf." What new behaviors would they have to practice? What new attitudes would they have? How would they behave differently? Students may wish to create individual posters outlining their plans for behavioral change.

4. Have students interview adults and other students in the school on the advantages and disadvantages of wearing glasses. The information can be compiled and presented in the form of an oversized chart hung on one wall of the classroom.

5. Invite selected students to try remaining silent for a predetermined length of time (an hour, for example). Afterward, have them discuss some of their frustrations at not being able to communicate verbally with others in the class. Can they invent other forms of communication to substitute for talking?

Science/Health

1. Invite an optometrist or ophthalmologist to discuss the care of eyes with your students. Have the speaker talk about how people see and what glasses actually do as an aid to good vision. Many eye doctors have brochures and leaflets on eye care that can be made available to students.

2. Check a science text or library resource and obtain a cutaway view of the human eye (many doctors have models of the human eye). Provide students with large styrofoam balls and tempera paints and ask them to create their own three-dimensional models of the human eye to display in the classroom. Slips of paper with the names of eye parts can be pinned to each model.

3. Invite the school nurse to administer a vision test to each child in the classroom. Provide each student with a written report of the vision test to take home to their parents.

4. Challenge students to collect as many different examples of leaves as they can. The object is not to collect a quantity of leaves, but rather one example of each different type of leaf. Have students observe each leaf and note the variations in shape, color, and size. Students can work together to create a leaf scrapbook by gluing individual leaves to sheets of paper and describing each leaf's characteristics and similarities in comparison to other leaves.

5. Have students investigate the different types of doctors. They can check the local Yellow Pages or listing for a hospital to determine the wide variety of medical specialists there are. They may wish to put together a dictionary of doctors along with a description of what each one does.

Art

1. Have students collect several different varieties of leaves from the local area. Instruct them on how to take leaf rubbings (place a piece of tracing paper over a leaf and rub over it with a pencil, preferably one with a soft lead). After students have made several rubbings, invite them to add different colors to represent the varieties of colors leaves can have during a single growing season. Have students arrange their rubbings into a scrapbook or bulletin-board display.

2. Provide students with examples of various types of advertisements (display ads, classified ads, Yellow Pages ads, magazine ads, etc.). Divide the class into several groups and have each group choose one of the ad types and develop an advertisement for a circus that is coming to town. After the various ads are completed, discuss the impact a colorful magazine-type ad has in comparison to a classified ad, for example. Which one would entice more people to attend the circus? Which one is most powerful? What kind of images are created with written ads versus illustrated ads?

Math

1. Direct students to hold pencil races on their desks (or some other appropriate surface) as Lucas did in the book. Have students obtain a variety of pencils (big, small, round, hexagonal) and roll them down a measured course. Record the average time it takes each type of pencil to roll (several trials with one type of pencil should be taken and then averaged). Have students record their data on a large chart for display in the classroom.

2. In the book, Arthur's teacher speaks of how excited she is that there is 100 percent attendance. Have your students compute the daily attendance rate for your class. Show students how to figure percentages (total number of students in the class divided into the number of students present). Have students maintain a monthly chart or calendar on which the daily percentage rate is recorded. At the end of each week (and the month), have students compute that average attendance rate and record it as well.

Music

1. In the book, Lucas made up a rhyme about his twin brother. Ask students to work together to collect examples of familiar and popular songs that have references to family members (brothers, sisters, grandmothers, fathers, aunts, etc.). Challenge students to collect the titles to as many family-orien ed songs as they can gather from radio, television, music class, and the like.

Social Studies

1. Divide the class into pairs of students. Assign each pair the name of one explorer mentioned in your social studies text. Each pair is responsible for putting together an entry for a classroom scrapbook about that explorer, including places visited, travels, famous facts, illustrations, and so on. As each explorer is encountered in the social studies text, the scrapbook entry can be used as supplemental material.

2. The National Geographic Society (Washington, DC) produces an outstanding sound filmstrip series entitled Great Explorers (1978 [catalog no. 03931]). Each of these four fifteen-minute filmstrips deals with one explorer: Christopher Columbus, Ferdinand Magellan, Sir Francis Drake, and Captain James Cook. After observing these filmstrips, students can be organized into four groups, with each group preparing a map of the travels and discoveries of one explorer (see activity 1 of this section).

3. The children in Lucas's classroom performed a circus play. Have your students investigate the history of the circus, some of the more traditional acts, the people who perform in the circus, and the kinds of animals that perform with the circus. Here are some sources to get them started: *At the Circus*, by Eugene Booth (Milwaukee, WI: Raintree, 1977) and *Let's Go to the Circus*, by Lisl Weil (New York: Holiday, 1988).

Physical Education

1. Introduce the art of mime to your students. Have students go through the motions associated with various activities (e.g., raking leaves, setting the table, cooking, playing football). Invite students to participate in groups and pantomime various types of classroom activities (e.g., going to lunch, getting ready for the school bus, etc.). Emphasize that mime is much more than just doing an activity without speaking—it is also a form of expression through control of muscles and body movements. Contact a local theater group and invite a local mime to demonstrate some techniques to your students.

DID YOU CARRY THE FLAG TODAY, CHARLIE?
Rebecca Caudill
New York: Holt, Rinehart and Winston, 1966

Summary:

Four-year-old Charlie begins Little School in the Appalachian Mountains. His nine older brothers and sisters say the highest honor is to be chosen to carry the flag at the end of the day. This honor is given to the student who has been most helpful throughout the day. Charlie, however, is too curious in his exploration of the new world around him to be chosen for the honor. Charlie does eventually get to carry the flag, but he realizes that learning new things is what excites him the most.

Critical Thinking Questions:

1. Why is it important for students to learn how to read? What would be some consequences for someone who did not know how to read?

2. What do you think would surprise Charlie if he came to visit your house?

3. Pretend that you are a rock. What kinds of things would you feel? How are those different or similar to the things you feel as a live organism?

4. The flag made the children feel special. What are some things in your classroom that make you feel special? What are some things at home that make you feel special?

5. How would you go about helping someone who could not read? What activities or materials would you recommend? Would it make any difference how old a person is? Why?

Reading/Language Arts

1. Have students interview their grandparents or the resident of a local nursing home or retirement village. Have students put together a questionnaire concerning schooling and schools in "the good old days." Students may also want to ask questions about what life was like without some of the modern conveniences (washing machine, indoor plumbing, iron, etc.) we take for granted today. Have students compare their responses with the lifestyles portrayed in the book.

2. Have students, working in pairs, choose an incident from the book. One child will retell this section of the story for the class and the other child will draw a picture to illustrate the part the reader is sharing.

3. Have students create a radio broadcast advertising the book. This may be tape recorded and presented over the school's intercom system.

4. Students may be interested in reading other books by the same author. For example, *A Pocketful of Cricket* (New York: Holt, 1964); *Contrary Jenkins* (New York: Holt, 1969); and *Wind, Sand, and Sky* (New York: Dutton, 1976).

Science/Health

1. To learn about sedimentary rocks, have students fill several mason jars one-third full with rocks, pebbles, sand, and dirt. Have students add water to the jars, cover them, and shake vigorously. Leave the jars undisturbed overnight. The next day students will notice that the coarser, heavier materials have settled on the bottom of the jars and the lighter materials are nearer the top. Explain that this is how sedimentary rocks get their start (pressure is also necessary).

2. Have students work in groups to select a species of snake and research it in the library. A list of snake species can be found on page 60 of the book (i.e., rattlesnake, copperhead, blue lace, garter, water moccasin, boa constrictor, king cobra, etc.). A good resource is *Amazing Snakes*, by Alexandra Parsons (an Eyewitness Junior Book) (New York: Knopf, 1990).

3. Take the class on a nature walk around your school or in the local community. Provide students with notebooks beforehand and encourage them to record everything they see on the walk. Later, back in the classroom, discuss all the observations that were made.

Art

1. Direct each student to create a "Me Flag" to promote individual self-esteem. Have students design their flags in any way they wish (you may wish to show samples of flags from various countries) and add their own illustrations, pictures, photos, or inscriptions. Flags can be made on construction paper or on sections cut from an old sheet. These should be displayed outside the classroom in the hallway or outside.

2. Have the class work together to create a "giant thing" like Charlie's in the book. Have students bring in several old tube socks and cut off the toe end of each. Sew the socks together to create one long tube. Have the class stuff the tube with fabric scraps or newspapers. They can then decorate their "thing" with paint, sequins, buttons, glitter, yarn, etc.

3. Have students make their own paper snakes. Lay out a full size, double-spread sheet of newsprint. Cut two narrow paper strips from the long edge. Weave the two paper strips by first overlapping the ends of each strip so that they are at right angles. Fold each strip over the other one at a time. Continue folding until the ends are reached. Glue the ends together. Gently stretch out the accordian-folded snake. Color and decorate.

Math

1. Obtain a map of the eastern United States and have students calculate the distance, in miles or kilometers, of the length of the Appalachian Mountains. Have them compare that distance with the length of other mountain ranges in the United States (i.e., Rocky Mountains, Cascades, Sierra Nevadas) or around the world (i.e., Alps, Himalayas, Andes).

2. Have students research the lengths of various species of snakes (see Science/Health activity 2). Ask students to chart that data in the form of bar graphs. Measurements may also be converted to inches, feet, yards, meters, centimeters, etc.

3. Bring several watermelons to class. Cut a watermelon into several sections width-wise. Cut one section in half, another into thirds, another into fourths, and so on to visually demonstrate fractions. Of course, students should be allowed to eat their fractions.

Music

1. Students may wish to create their own jug band. Instruments can include:

   Jug (a large bottle—sound is created by blowing across the top of the opening)

   Washtub bass (turn an old metal washtub upside down, punch a hole in the bottom, thread nylon line through the hole and tie the end to a washer. Notch one end of an old broom handle and place it over the edge of the tub. Attach the line to the top of the pole, stretching the line tightly. Pluck the line to create sound)

   Musical comb (a piece of waxed paper is placed behind a comb and the player hums against the paper)

   Spoons (two spoons held together, back to back, and hit against the body)

2. Students will enjoy listening to different samples of bluegrass music. Popular artists include The Dillards, Flatt and Scruggs, Doc Watson, and Pete Seeger. Recordings can be obtained through your school or local public library.

Social Studies

1. The National Geographic Society (Washington, DC) has a fifteen-minute video entitled *Portrait of a Coal Miner* (1980 [catalog no. 51175]) that is a good introduction to coal and its mining for those students not familiar with this industry. A good book on coal and mining is *Coal*, by Betsy Harvey (New York: Watts, 1976).

2. Your students may be interested in obtaining a catalog of U.S. and foreign flags. One can be obtained (free of charge) from A Signers Flag and Flagpoles (221 Old Delp Road, Lancaster, PA; 800-872-5638).

3. Using a map of the United States, have students locate the Appalachian Mountains. Have students note the states the Appalachians pass through. Students can be formed into groups to research each of those states. Information can be obtained by writing to the Department of Tourism for a particular state. For example:

   Travel West Virginia, 2101 Washington Street, Charleston, WV 25305

   Division of Tourism, 202 North 9th Street, Richmond, VA 23219

   Department of Tourism, 2200 Capital Plaza Tower, Frankfort, KY 40601

   Travel and Tourism Division, 430 North Salisbury Street, Raleigh, NC 27611

   Department of Tourist Development, Box 23170, Nashville, TN 37202

4. Contact your local literacy council (listed in the telephone book) or International Reading Association reading council. They may be able to provide a speaker to talk to your students about efforts to promote literacy throughout the community. The speaker should provide data on the ramifications of illiteracy and its implications for individuals.

Physical Education

1. Students may enjoy trying some clog dancing. A single clog step-shuffle is a quick short movement of the foot brushing the toe of the foot back and forth before stepping on it. Alternate feet and move forward as follows: Shuffle with right foot; drop or step onto right foot while slightly bending knee; shuffle with left foot; drop or step onto left foot while slightly bending knee; repeat. Check with your local library for the recording "Appalachian Clog Dancing and Big Circle Mountain Square Dancing" by Glenn Bannerman (Freeport, NY: Educational Activities, Inc., n.d.).

2. Have a shoe relay. Divide the class into two teams and provide each team with a bucket. The first person in each team runs to a designated spot with the bucket, takes off his or her shoes, puts them in the bucket, runs back to the team, dumps the shoes in a pile, and gives the bucket to the next team member. Each team member follows the same sequence. After the last team member returns, everyone retrieves their shoes from the pile, puts them on, and sits down. The first team to complete all these actions is the winner.

EAST OF THE SUN AND WEST OF THE MOON
Mercer Mayer
New York: Macmillan, 1980

Summary:

The beautiful daughter of a farmer faces hardship when her father becomes ill and she must seek water from the South Wind. A frog assists her in return for three wishes. When the frog wishes to marry her, she refuses and kills the frog. A spell is broken and the frog turns into a handsome youth who is taken away to the Land of East of the Sun and West of the Moon to wed the Troll Princess. The maiden travels in search of her love with the help of enchanting creatures along the way.

Critical Thinking Questions:

1. What would have happened if the maiden had turned into a frog? What would the youth have done?

2. What would you do if a frog asked you to marry it? Would you react in the same way the maiden did?

3. The frog was allowed three wishes, but only asked two. What would have been the third wish?

4. How would the story have been different if the youth had not been a frog, but another animal such as a cat, rabbit, or giraffe?

5. Where is the Land of East of the Sun and West of the Moon?

6. Is it important always to keep a promise? Why or why not?

Reading/Language Arts

1. Contact your school or local public library and make arrangements for a storyteller to visit your classroom (your local Yellow Pages may also list a storytelling guild or association in your area). Have the storyteller share stories in the same genre as *East of the Sun*.

2. To reinforce how folktales are passed down from generation to generation, divide the class into several groups and direct each group to create its own original folktale. Have each group tape record their tale and preserve it in a special location. Several months later, ask group members to recall the specifics of their folktale, then play the recording of their original story. Discuss the changes that occurred between the two tellings. Let students know that these changes are a normal and natural part of storytelling that give folktales their special flavor and design.

3. In a class discussion, have students determine when important events took place. Have students record events on a time line to reinforce the sequential development of the story line. Here is an example of a simple time line:

Maiden   Frog   Salamander   Forest   Fish   Troll   Marriage

4. Read *The Frog Prince*, by Jane White Canfield (New York: Harper, 1970). As a class discussion, have students list similarities and differences between the two stories. This can be done by using two semantic webs, one for each story. Details for each story can be listed on its appropriate semantic web.

5. Have students check the library for other versions of this story.

Science/Health

1. Students may wish to grow their own frogs. Kits are available from Holcombs Educational Materials (3205 Harvard Avenue, Cleveland, OH 44105; 800-321-2543). Kit 998-0215H is priced at $14.95 (at this writing) and includes a container, food, instructions, and a coupon for live tadpoles. You may also wish to check your local teacher supply store for similar kits.

2. Show the video *Tadpoles and Frogs* (Washington, DC: National Geographic Society, 1979 [catalog no. 51218]) to your class. Discuss the growth and development of frogs from tadpoles to adults.

3. Have students make a list of all the real animals in the book and another list of all the fictitious animals. Have students examine the list of fictitious animals to determine the real animals that would closely resemble each fictitious animal. For example, Gila monsters and Komodo dragons are real-life equivalents of the giant salamander. This information can be charted and shared with the class in the form of an oral report, pictures, or a display.

4. Provide students with a copy of the Beaufort Wind Speed chart (most science texts have one). Make arrangements to call a local weather station or the meteorologist at a local college daily to determine the average wind speed for the day. Have students record these speeds on a specially designed monthly calendar.

Art

1. Students may wish to build their own version of a troll palace. Have students bring in recycled materials such as milk cartons, cereal boxes, tin cans, and bottles. Glue, paint, string, and other art materials can be provided, along with a scheduled period of time and encouragement of imagination, for completion of the project.

2. Students can create trolls from homemade clay. Here's a recipe:

   1 cup flour
   ½ cup salt
   ⅓ cup water

   Mix flour and salt. Add water, a little at a time. Squeeze the dough until it is smooth. Form into shapes. Let air dry or bake at 225 degrees for 30 minutes. Paint with tempera paints. (Note: Adjust the recipe according to the number of students participating.)

3. Have students make their own wind socks. Form strips of construction paper into cylinders and attach colored streamers of tissue paper to the sides of the cylinders. Punch two holes near one end of the cylinder, one on top and one on the bottom, and insert a wooden dowel (the cylinder should spin freely on the dowel). Stick a pin through the dowel to serve as a resting place for the cylinder. Have students go outside and hold their wind socks in the wind or poke the dowels into the ground for a colorful display.

Math

1. Have students convert U.S. currency into Norwegian currency. (At this writing a Norwegian krone is worth fourteen cents; check with your local bank for current exchange rates.) Have students determine how much a favorite fast-food meal would cost in kroner.

2. Have students survey all the other students who have read this book. Have students make lists of all the characters in the book and question others about who their favorite character is. Have students tabulate the results and present them in the form of bar graphs, pie charts, or line graphs.

3. Have students list all the animals in the book and categorize those animals from smallest to largest.

Music

1. Have students learn the traditional folk song "A Frog Went A-Courtin'." One version can be found in *Go In and Out the Window*, music arranged by Dan Fox (New York: Henry Holt and Co., 1987). After students learn the song, they may wish to add some sound effects (frog and mouse sounds).

2. Have students create a wedding dance. Children can stand in a circle, some with tambourines and recorders to provide background music. A piece of recorded classical music can also be used.

3. Students may wish to make their own recorders or flutes and invent an appropriate accompanying song for the book. Directions for making all sorts of musical instruments can be found in *Making Musical Things*, by Ann Wiseman (New York: Charles Scribner's Sons, 1979).

Social Studies

1. In group discussions, have students list real places or things on earth that resemble the fictitious places in the story. For example, "Mountain of Ice" could be the Antarctic, "Father Forest" could be Olympic National Forest, "Great Fish of the Sea" could be whales or manatees. Have students form small groups and select one area to research. A display for each area can be set up in the classroom to include maps, drawings, photographs, pictures, stories, and facts.

2. To further appreciate "Father Forest," students may wish to contact the following organizations for materials and information regarding forests and forest conservation:

    National Arbor Day Foundation, 100 Arbor Avenue, Nebraska City, NE 68410;

    National Wildlife Federation, 1400 16th Street, NW, Washington, DC 20036;

    Save America's Forests, 4 Library Court, SE, Washington, DC 20003;

    Native Forest Action Council, P.O. Box 2176, Eugene, OR 97402;

    Lighthawk, P.O. Box 8163, Santa Fe, NM 87504.

    Information gathered from these organizations can be used as a bulletin-board display or a classroom learning center.

3. Some students may be interested in researching the Vikings and their explorations. The information gathered from their research can be presented to the class in the form of an oral report.

Physical Education

1. Students may enjoy engaging in an obstacle course relay race replicating the maiden's travels. For example: Ice—carry ice cubes on spoons; Swim—wiggle on mat to designated area; Wind—blow a balloon along the floor; Troll—bean bag toss at a picture of a troll.

2. Have students play a game of "Leapfrog" over a designated course laid out on the playground.

THE FALLEN SPACEMAN
Lee Harding
New York: Bantam-Skylark Books, 1973

Summary:

By accident Tyro, a spaceman, falls to Earth. He has no way of knowing if his own people realize what has happened to him or if they will be able to rescue him. The adventure continues when he takes on Erik, an Earth boy, as a passenger on his spaceship. The result: two trapped and frightened travelers.

Critical Thinking Questions:

1. Do you believe there is intelligent life on other planets? Why do you believe as you do? What proof do you have?

2. Why was Erik not afraid? Would you have been afraid, given the same set of circumstances?

3. Why do you think Tyro was willing to give up his life for Erik? Is there someone in your family or class you would be willing to give up your life for?

4. What would you do if you encountered an alien? Would you behave any differently if you encountered a person from a foreign country?

5. If you could talk to Tyro, what would you most want to tell him?

Reading/Language Arts

1. Ask students to discuss what might have happened if Tyro's people had not come back to take him home. Would he have died? Would scientists have created a special breathing machine for him? Later, invite students to write a new ending for the book based on their discussions.

2. Ask students to make individual lists of some of the times they have been afraid. Then ask students to work in groups to determine if group members share any common experiences, that is, frightening experiences that happen to many people (e.g., going to the dentist, watching a scary movie, etc.). Each group can then prepare a guidebook for younger students on the types of frightening experiences they can expect to encounter in their lives and how they can prepare for those experiences. For example, what kinds of advice would students give to prepare a younger child for riding a particular type of amusement ride?

3. Divide the class into several groups. Have some of the groups take on the role of Erik while other groups take on the role of Tyro. Invite the groups to establish a pen pal system between these two major characters. Have Tyro write a letter to Erik one day and have Erik respond with a letter to Tyro the next day. Have the pen pals continue writing for several days.

4. Erik and Tyro were unable to speak to one another. Use this situation to introduce your students to sign language. Here are two books to get your students started: *My First Book of Sign*, by Pamela Baker (Washington, DC: Gallaudet University Press, 1986) and *I Can Sign My ABC's*, by Susan Chaplin (Washington, DC: Gallaudet University Press, 1986). Have students learn some simple signs and attempt to communicate with one another. Invite students to discuss the difficulties they encounter with this form of language.

Science/Health

1. Have students conduct a simple experiment to learn why oxygen is important to all living things on earth. Obtain two identical insects (grasshopper, cricket, fly) and place one in a sealed container (a mason jar with a screw-on top) and another in a jar with holes punched in the lid. Have students observe the actions and reactions of the two insects over a period of several days. How can they account for the differences? Would lack of oxygen account for those differences?

2. Introduce your students to space travel. Here are some books to get them started: *Flying to the Moon and Other Strange Places*, by Michael Collins (New York: Farrar, 1976); *First Travel Guide to the Moon: What to Pack, How to Go, and What to See When You Get There*, by Rhoda Blumberg (New York: Four Winds, 1980); and *Finding Out about Rockets and Spaceflight*, by Lynn Myring (New York: Usborne, 1982).

3. Provide students with styrofoam balls of varying sizes, some thread or yarn, and different colors of tempera paints. Direct them to research the planets in our solar system and to create a replica of the solar system using the materials. This replica can be displayed in a corner of the room and referred to during the appropriate time in science class.

4. Ask students to observe the phases of the moon over a period of several days (a month, for example). Have students record on a large chart or oversize calendar the phase of the moon for each day of the month. Encourage children to make predictions on the anticipated moon phases for the following month.

5. Have students investigate the role of women in space exploration and travel. The following books will provide students with some fascinating information: *Sally Ride: America's First Woman in Space*, by Carolyn Blacknall (Minneapolis, MN: Dillan Press, 1984); *Women in Space: Reaching the Last Frontier*, by Carole Briggs (Minneapolis, MN: Lerner, 1987); and *Christa McAuliffe*, by Charlene Billings (Hillside, NJ: Enslow, 1986).

Art

1. Provide students with modeling clay or supplies for making papier-mâché. Ask them to create models or replicas of various types of spacecraft, both real and imaginary. Have students arrange their models into an attractive display. You may also wish to share with them *Drawing Spaceships and Other Spacecraft*, by Don Bolognese (New York: Watts, 1982).

2. Invite small groups of students to draw what they think Tyro looks like. Ask them to read over the description of Tyro in the book and decide on the dimensions and features of the alien. After each group has completed its illustrations, have the groups compare their drawings. Have the groups discuss the similarities and differences between and among their drawings.

Math

1. The force of gravity on the moon is one-sixth that on Earth. Have students weight various objects in the classroom (even themselves) and compute how much those same objects would weigh on the moon.

2. The length of a year (in Earth time) is different on each of the planets in our solar system as indicated in the following chart:

Mercury	88 days
Venus	225 days
Mars	687 days
Jupiter	11.9 years
Saturn	29.5 years
Uranus	84 years
Neptune	164 years
Pluto	247 years

Using the data in this chart or from independent library research, have students compute the length of summer, the length of a week, or the length of the football season on each of the planets in our solar system.

Music

1. Have students listen to *Also Sprach Zarathustra* (best known for its use as the theme from the movie *2001: A Space Odyssey* [MGM Records, no. MGL-513]). Ask them to speculate why this music was chosen as the theme music for a movie about space travel. Have students listen to other portions of the sound track and speculate on the actions or activities that might be taking place in the movie, based solely on the music they hear.

Social Studies

1. Have students work together in small groups to create a list of products or objects that have been named for objects in the solar system, for example, the *Milky Way* candy bar, Mickey Mouse's dog *Pluto*, and the *Saturn* car. Ask students to speculate why these names have been used.

2. Ask students to investigate alternative fuel sources for various forms of transportation. For example, solar-powered cars, electromagnetic trains, and nuclear-powered ships. What are the implications of these fuel sources for future generations?

3. Have students investigate the locating and naming of constellations done by the Greeks and Romans. What is the historical significance of these names? How did the constellations influence life in those times? An excellent resource is *The Constellations*, by Roy A. Gallant (New York: Four Winds, 1979).

4. Place students in several groups and assign each group one topic dealing with space exploration. One group could investigate the space race between the United States and the Soviet Union. Another group could look into early manned flights (the Mercury program). Another group could research the flights to and exploration of the moon. Still another group could read about the space shuttle program and the future of space flight. The data from these investigations can be combined into a class notebook for future reference.

Physical Education

1. Keeping physically fit is difficult for space travelers because of the lack of gravity. Share the book *To Space and Back*, by Sally Ride and Susan Okie (New York: Lothrop, 1986), particularly the parts about life in zero gravity. Ask students to develop a series of exercises or activities for astronauts that would help keep them in shape in a zero-gravity environment.

THE HALF-A-MOON INN
Paul Fleischman
New York: Harper and Row, 1980

Summary:

Aaron, a mute boy, begins to mature on the day before his twelfth birthday. Left alone by his mother, who does not return on time, the boy sets out in search for her. He meets an array of strangers who convince him that good can prevail over evil.

Critical Thinking Questions:

1. How would you feel if you could not talk with anyone? How would your life change or be different?

2. What advantages do you think a mute person might have? What disadvantages?

3. The book is a story about good triumphing over evil. How would you apply that idea to your own life? Specifically, what personal event(s) would prove that to be a true statement?

4. If you were Aaron, what would you buy with the reward money?

5. What part of your personality do you think people would like to know more about? What part of your personality would you like to share with others?

Reading/Language Arts

1. Students will want to read other books by this author, such as: *Rondo in C* (New York: Harper and Row, 1988); *Graven Images* (New York: Harper and Row, 1982); *I Am Phoenix: Poems for Two Voices* (New York: Harper and Row, 1985); *Joyful Noise: Poems for Two Voices* (New York: Harper and Row, 1988); *Coming-and-Going Men: Four Tales* (New York: Harper and Row, 1985); and *Path of the Pale Horse* (New York: Harper and Row, 1983).

2. Have students ask their parents for help in locating various recipes for potato soup. If a student cannot locate one at home, consult the library or make one up. Have students bring their recipes to school and transcribe them into a *Potato Soup Recipe Book*. Make sure the book is put on display in the library.

3. Designate half of a particular day as "No Talking Day." Invite students to develop other forms of communication to be used during this period so that individuals and groups can interact with one another. After the designated time period is finished, encourage students to discuss some of the difficulties or challenges they encountered.

Science/Health

1. Check the telephone book for the name of a local weaver's guild, fabric shop, or sheep farm. Try to obtain a sample of raw wool to bring to the class. Have students compare the texture of the raw wool to the texture of

wool clothes they may be wearing. What differences do they note? Students may be interested in researching sheep: how they grow and develop, their commercial uses, the sheep industry in this country and New Zealand, and the care and feeding of sheep.

2. Provide students with several unbreakable thermometers and ask them to take their temperatures once every hour over the course of a day (be sure the thermometers are sterilized with alcohol after each use). Have individuals keep a record of each of their personal readings (which can be recorded on a graph). Although normal body temperature for humans is 98.6 degrees, some students will note that body temperature fluctuates during the day. Ask students to speculate on reasons for the differences.

3. An excellent series of sound filmstrips on the human body is produced by the National Geographic Society. This series of four filmstrips, entitled Inside Your Body (1984 [catalog no. 04719]), includes informative data on growth and change, how bones and muscles work, respiration and digestion, and the human brain. It is a wonderful supplement to discussions on Aaron and the events surrounding the blizzard.

Art

1. Have students create a series of business signs or safety signs that use illustrations in place of words or phrases. For example, a barber shop could be designated with a series of twisting strips, a motel by a picture of a person in bed, a "Do Not Cross" sign by an "X" over an illustration of a person walking. Encourage students to design their own original signs for situations and shops that do not presently have signs.

2. Obtain a box of Popsicle™ sticks from a local art store. Invite students to create a replica of the Half-a-Moon Inn using the sticks, white glue, and a variety of tempera paints.

Math

1. Obtain several menus from restaurants in your area. Divide the class into several small groups and provide each group with a menu. Have group members decide on the items they would like to order if they were to visit that particular restaurant. Then ask each group to total the prices of the meals ordered by all the members of the group. Have each group also compute a 15 percent tip for the server as well.

2. Call several motels or hotels in your area and obtain their rates for singles, doubles, and suites. Have students compute the charges for various individuals and groups staying at a particular motel. For example, a single businessperson, a husband and wife, a family of four with one baby and one eleven-year-old, or a couple over the age of sixty-five. Since some hotels add sales tax, students should calculate the total bill. Other establishments are also required to add in an occupancy tax (usually 9 percent to 12 percent) on top of the total bill, which students can figure out, too.

Music

1. Write for a catalog from Weston Woods (Weston, CT 06880) a company that produces an excellent series of sound filmstrips of popular and traditional folk songs. Your school, public, or local college library will probably have some of their recordings to play in your class. The catalog of Educational Activities (P.O. Box 392, Freeport, NY 11520) also includes traditional folk songs.

Social Studies

1. Invite a sociologist or home economics professor from a local college to visit your classroom to explain the changes taking place in families. Ask the visitor to describe family life as it was 100 or 200 years ago in comparison with

family life today. What are some of the more notable changes? How has the structure of the family been altered? What is a nuclear family?

2. Invite students to set up their own individual family trees. Have students trace their family lines back two or more generations, if possible, listing their parents, grandparents, and great-grandparents. Be especially sensitive to foster children and adopted children, who should be given the option of tracing their natural, adopted, or temporary family, as they choose.

3. Have students look into the history and influence of sailing vessels over the years. How many different types of sailing ships are there? What influence did they have in exploration and trade? Students may wish to create a fictitious diary of a sailor on a square rigger, a scrapbook of illustrations and photographs of various sailing vessels, a description of some of the most famous sailing ships, or replicas of maps outlining trade routes and voyages of discovery.

Physical Education

1. Place an assortment of old silverware on a desk or table some distance from a group of students. Have each student run to the table, set it with the silverware, and run back to a designated spot. Record the times for each individual. This event can also be scheduled as a team relay, too. In the team event, each runner must set a different place at a table and run back to tag the next runner. The team that finishes first is the winner.

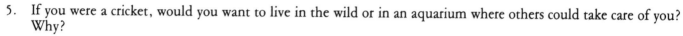

MUCH ADO ABOUT ALDO
Johanna Hurwitz
New York: Morrow, 1978

Summary:

Aldo is interested in everything. One day, the teacher sets up an aquarium in which she places crickets and chameleons together at the same time. The sensitivity that Aldo shows toward the crickets causes him not only to hide the chameleons in the teacher's desk drawer, but also to make the decision to become a vegetarian. Eventually, Aldo has the opportunity to explain his feelings to all.

Critical Thinking Questions:

1. If you could have any animal you wanted as a pet, which one would you choose? Why do you think that animal would make the best pet?

2. If you were Aldo, where would you have hidden the chameleons, other than in the desk drawer?

3. How long do you think you would be able to go without eating meat, as Aldo did in the story?

4. If it were possible for you to decide on the number of brothers and sisters you could have in your house, how many of each would you choose? Explain why.

5. If you were a cricket, would you want to live in the wild or in an aquarium where others could take care of you? Why?

Reading/Language Arts

1. Students will enjoy reading other books by this author, such as *Super Duper Teddy* (New York: Morrow, 1980); *Russell and Elisa* (New York: Morrow, 1989); and *Yellow Blue Jay* (New York: Morrow, 1986).

2. Present students with the scenario that their cat or dog has run away. Ask them each to record their feelings in a journal or notebook. Later, ask students to share their feelings and discuss any similarities and differences in how they felt.

3. Have students create a "Wanted" poster for Aldo's cat. What type of information should be placed on the poster? Will a reward be offered?

4. Bring in several telephone books and direct students to collect a list of agencies, organizations, and businesses that deal with cats. Have students put together a small version of the phone book with information specifically about cats. How many different people, groups, and organizations provide cat services? Why are there so many listings for or about cats?

Science/Health

1. Obtain an old aquarium (at a pet store or yard sale) or several very large glass jars. Fill them with rocks and pebbles, sticks, and a few small plants. Purchase some crickets at a local pet store (one pet store in my area sells

crickets at 15 for $1.00) and place some in each of the containers (be careful of overcrowding). Have students observe and record the habits of the crickets over a period of time.

2. Students may enjoy reading some books about crickets and chameleons. Check with the school librarian or start off with these suggestions: *A Pocketful of Cricket*, by Rebecca Caudill (New York: Holt, 1964); *Why Worry?*, by Eric Kimmel (New York: Pantheon, 1979); *If I Were a Cricket*, by Kazue Mizumara (New York: Crowell, 1973); *The Mixed-Up Chameleon*, by Eric Carle (New York: Crowell, 1975); and *Chameleon the Spy and the Terrible Toaster Trap*, by Diane Massie (New York: Crowell, 1982). Some of the suggestions are fiction and others are nonfiction. Ask students to compare and contrast the actual facts about crickets and chameleons with the fictionalized accounts. How do they account for any discrepancies?

3. Discuss the diet a vegetarian eats. Challenge students to put together a daily menu for a vegetarian (breakfast, lunch, dinner). If you know any vegetarians, ask them to share information with your students on the foods eaten and not eaten.

4. The National Geographic Society (Washington, DC) has five sound filmstrips in the series Animals and How They Grow (1976 [catalog no. 03777]). Three of the filmstrips—*Amphibians and Reptiles*, *Mammals*, and *Insects*—cover the characteristics and growth patterns of these groups of animals. Try to obtain these filmstrips for showing to your class.

Art

1. Ask small groups of students each to make three different collages. One collage would consist of pictures and illustrations of favorite insects; another collage would include pictures and illustrations of favorite reptiles; and the third collage would consist of pictures of favorite mammals. Post these around the classroom.

2. Have students design papier-mâché or modeling clay replicas of crickets and chameleons to be placed around the room or in a facsimile of a terrarium.

Math

1. Have students check with a local veterinarian (or conduct library research) on the life expectancy of some of their favorite animals. Have students gather this data in the form of charts or graphs to compare the life spans of various creatures.

2. As part of activity 1, students may be interested in computing the age conversion factor for various animals. For example, one human year equals seven "dog" years. When students have collected several examples, ask them to devise their own word problems for selected animals (e.g., if a dog is eight human years old, how many dog years does that equal?).

3. Ask students to discover the different dimensions of the animals mentioned in the story. An oversized chart can be set up along one wall of the classroom comparing height, weight, and length of selected animals.

Music

1. There are many songs about animals. Your students may wish to put together a collection of titles of songs that have something to do with animals. Songs such as "Blue Tail Fly," "Poor Butterfly," and "Puff, The Magic Dragon" might be appropriate. See *Family Songbook*, music arranged and edited by Dan Fox (Pleasantville, NY: Reader's Digest Association, 1969).

Social Studies

1. Have students interview a variety of adults about the types of pets or animals they grew up with as children. Have the students compile their data in summary form. Then ask students to interview a representative sample of classmates or age-mates. Do they notice any differences or similarities between the two lists? How do they account for any differences? What social conditions might account for the differences?

2. Divide the class into several small groups for library research. Have each group select one country and put together a compendium of foods common to the people of that country. How can they account for the differences in traditional foods? Is climate a factor? Are social conditions a factor? How can they account for the fact that some countries tend to have more starches in their diet while others have more vegetables? Students may wish to create small brochures on the foodstuffs of particular countries.

Physical Education

1. Have students play a game of kickball. However, in this version they must take on the role of a cricket, chameleon, or cat and must kick and run on all fours. Later, have students discuss any difficulties they had in playing kickball on four appendages versus playing it with just two appendages.

2. Have students imagine that they are living in a cage or terrarium (place masking tape in the shape of a small square on part of the classroom floor to simulate a cage or terrarium; a 4-by-4-foot square might be appropriate). Ask students to design an appropriate exercise program for staying in shape if they had to inhabit such a space for a long period of time.

SHOESHINE GIRL
Clyde Robert Bulla
New York: Crowell, 1975

Summary:

Sarah Ida, a ten-year-old city girl, is sent to live with her aunt Claudia in a rural area for the summer. Sarah's parents are afraid that she is hanging out with the wrong type of people. Not accustomed to this new way of living, Sarah starts off on the wrong foot, but by the end of her stay, she learns the true meaning of friendship.

Critical Thinking Questions:

1. What do you think Sarah's parents should have done with her? Do you agree or disagree with what they did? Why?

2. What do you think was the most important lesson Sarah learned? Given the same set of circumstances, would you have learned the same lesson?

3. Why was it so difficult for Sarah to talk with anyone? Why are people generally afraid to talk with others?

4. How would you have reacted if you were Sarah?

5. Is Sarah someone you would like to have as a friend? As a next-door neighbor? As a classmate? Why?

Reading/Language Arts

1. Have students investigate the history of trains and the various types of trains there are in the world. They may wish to gather their data into a booklet that can be duplicated and distributed around the school. Some resources to get students started include: *The Freight Train Book*, by Jack Pierce (Minneapolis, MN: Carolrhoda, 1980); *Trains*, by Byron Barton (New York: Crowell, 1986); *The Train*, by Ray Marshall (New York: Viking, 1986); *Freight Trains*, by William Bunce (New York: Putnam, 1954); and *Trains*, by Gail Gibbons (New York: Holiday, 1987).

2. Have students bring shoeshining equipment to the class and practice the steps necessary to properly shine shoes. Later, have small groups of students each prepare an instructional booklet entitled "How to Shine Shoes." Have students compare and contrast the various editions.

3. Have students prepare an instructional poster or chart on how to conduct oneself during a job interview. They should include information on what to wear, what to say, how to act, and other instructions essential to getting a job. You may wish to invite an employer from a local business to discuss interview techniques with your students, too.

4. Have students make up a classified advertisement section for a fictitious newspaper. The classified ads in the paper will all deal with classroom jobs and chores. Have students develop one or more ads for the traditional jobs students do in the classroom. Provide students with examples from the local newspaper to use as references.

5. Students will want to read other books by this author, such as *A Lion to Guard Us* (New York: Crowell, 1981); *Squanto: Friend of the Pilgrims* (New York: Scholastic, 1971); *The Sword in the Tree* (New York: Crowell, 1956); and *Viking Adventure* (New York: Crowell, 1963).

Science/Health

1. Have students create a series of posters concerning safety at home, in the community, and at school. Students can work in small groups and hang their finished posters around the school.

2. Invite a paramedic from a local ambulance service to visit the class and explain some of the procedures used in that job. What kind of special training is necessary to become a paramedic? How are certain types of injuries treated? What are some of the typical accidents treated by a paramedic?

3. The National Geographic Society (Washington, DC) produces a series of five sound filmstrips entitled The Seasons (1975 [catalog no. 03765]). Filmstrip 3, *Summer*, traces the ways in which living things respond to the long days of summer. Obtain a copy and, after watching it, have students trace some of the ways in which their summer activities are similar to the activities of animals portrayed in the filmstrip. How are their activities different?

Art

1. Ask students to bring in old aprons from home or used ones obtained from a local thrift shop. Invite students to decorate their aprons in any way they wish. Materials can include yarn, sequins, ribbons, paints, buttons, etc. Challenge students to create the most unusual, most functional, or prettiest apron.

2. Have students design and illustrate special certificates of accomplishment that they would like to receive for classroom chores. The emphasis should be on the accomplishment of a job, not on who is best or completes a task first. Discuss with students the illustrations and words that could be used on these certificates.

Math

1. Invite students to create their own word problems using Sarah and her work shining shoes. For example, if Sarah charges 50 cents for each shoeshine, how many shoes will she have to shine to make $6.50?

2. Students can also create their own word problems using forms of transportation. For example, how long will it take a car going 50 mph to reach a destination 250 miles away? How much faster would it be if a person were to take a train going 100 mph?

Music

1. Have students write some original lyrics to the tune of "I've Been Working on the Railroad." They can call their song "I've Been Working on a Shoeshine."

2. Invite the music teacher or other musician from your area (contact a local music store) to demonstrate the mouth harp (harmonica) for your students. Ask the individual to play some traditional American ballads, particularly those relating to trains and train travel.

Social Studies

1. Hold a classroom forum on homelessness in this country. Ask students to discuss their perceptions of this problem and what can be done about it. Invite a local community worker or representative from a social agency to talk about the nature of homelessness in your community or in a nearby city.

2. An excellent video on life in the country is *Portrait of a Wheat Farmer* (Washington, DC: National Geographic Society, 1980 [catalog no. 51179]). This film serves as a fine introduction to the book and a focal point for class discussions on rural living.

3. Another excellent video is *Love Those Trains* (Washington, DC: National Geographic Society, n.d. [catalog no. 51382]), which takes a look at trains and train travel across the country. Use this film as another point of discussion for the book.

4. Ask students to conduct some library research on life in a one-room schoolhouse. What are some of the similarities and differences between that type of educational experience and the way students go to school today? Students can compile their data into their own video production (with actors, costumes, props, etc.) about education in the one-room schoolhouse.

Physical Education

1. Conduct a shoeshine race. Divide the class into teams of four. Set up pairs of shoes and sufficient shoeshining equipment along one wall of the classroom or one side of the playground. The first person in a team races to the designated spot, shines one shoe, and races back. The second person races to the spot, shines the other shoe, and races back. The third person races to the spot, puts the shoes in a box and races back with the shoes. The fourth person races to the spot, gathers the equipment, and races back with the equipment. The first team to finish is declared the winner.

THE WHIPPING BOY
Sid Fleischman
New York: Greenwillow, 1986

Summary:

Jemmy, who must be whipped every time the prince gets into trouble, leads the young royal through the forests and sewers of old England in an adventure filled with suspense, strange characters, and the coming of age of "Prince Brat."

Critical Thinking Questions:

1. What would you enjoy most about living during the time Jemmy and Prince Brat did? Why?

2. Is Prince Brat similar to anyone you know? In what ways?

3. What types of adventures do you think the two boys would get into in a sequel to this story?

4. How would Prince Brat's inability to read have been a problem for him later in life?

5. Describe what you would need to live in a sewer.

Reading/Language Arts

1. Have students suggest some ideas or strategies that would help the young prince learn to read. What do students do during their reading lessons that would be helpful to the prince?

2. Direct several students to write a sequel to the story. What kinds of new adventures would the two young boys get into now? Would their friendship blossom, or would they fall back into their old, familiar ways?

3. Have students check the local Yellow Pages for modern-day services that might be used by royalty. Examples may include carpet-cleaning services (for the red carpet), butlers, cooks, transportation services, etc.

4. Have students pretend they are news reporters covering the kidnapping of the prince. What facts or details would they want to include in a television broadcast? Which ones would be appropriate for a newspaper article?

Science/Health

1. Have several students investigate the life cycle of one of the animals mentioned in the story (e.g., horse, bear, cow, rat). This information can be assembled into a poster or an oral report shared with the class.

2. Have students investigate fog. What is it, how is it created, and what effects does it have on our daily lives?

3. Provide students with small slices of garlic, onion, potato, and apple and ask them to taste each one. What differences or similarities do they note? Afterward, blindfold several students and ask them to hold their noses. Give each student slices of the same items as before, but in random order. Ask each student to explain why it was difficult to distinguish the different items.

4. Have students investigate differences in sanitation during the time of this story and modern times. How do we take care of the disposal of our wastes in comparison with how wastes were disposed of years ago? Why is sanitation such an important urban and environmental issue?

Art

1. Have students create an animal collage by cutting out various pictures of cows, rats, horses, and bears from nature or environmental magazines. The pictures can be posted on sheets of construction paper and displayed throughout the room.

2. Students may wish to create a line of greeting cards that could have been used by characters in the story. For example, what type of card would Billy and Cutwater send to the king? What type of card would the prince want to send his father at the end of the story?

3. Have students create imaginary advertisements for some of the characters at the fair. Have students imagine that each character was going to put an ad in the local newspaper. What information should be included in each ad to attract more business?

Math

1. Have students locate various dimensions of the animals mentioned in the story. For example, what is the average weight of a rat? How long is it? How tall? This information can be graphed on a sheet of oaktag.

2. Some students may wish to investigate the differences between the old English monetary system and the American monetary system. What differences and similarities are there?

3. Bring in a large bag of potatoes and have students practice addition or multiplication facts using potatoes in various arrangements and sets.

4. Ask students to locate current prices on some of the items mentioned in the story. For example, how much does a bar of soap cost? A bag of potatoes? A horse? A clove of garlic? To what do they attribute the variations in prices?

Music

1. Demonstrate for students how various instruments can be used to imitate the motions or movements of various animals. For example, a flute can be used to depict a bird; a tuba can depict a bear. You may find it helpful to play recordings of *Peter and the Wolf* and *Carnival of the Animals* so that students can hear how different instruments suggest various animals.

2. Have students create or put together various homemade instruments that could be used in a retelling of the story. For example, two coconut shells pounded on a hard surface would provide the sound of a horse. Two sandpaper blocks rubbed together can imitate the sound of the boys walking slowly through the fog-shrouded forest. Rubbing wet fingers around the rim of a glass could imitate the sound of the sewer rats.

3. Students may enjoy listening to the record *The Lady and the Unicorn*, by John Renbourn (Warner Bros., 1970) a collection of medieval music, folk tunes, and other early music arranged for guitars, sitar, hand drums, glockenspiel, viola, concertina, flutes, and violin.

Social Studies

1. Have students look up the history of fairs and carnivals. How have they changed over the years? What events at today's fairs are identical to those of fairs long ago?

2. Direct students to construct an imaginary map of the prince's kingdom. Be sure to have them include all the sites mentioned in the story as well as any others they think would be important in a kingdom.

3. Have students investigate the different types of clothes worn by people during the time of this story. What kinds of clothes did rich people wear? What kinds of clothes were worn by poor people? What differences were there?

4. Ask students to collect several copies of travel magazines and prepare one description of England as it was in the time of this story and another description of England as it exists today. How do these two descriptions compare?

Physical Education

1. Have students invent various activities that would allow sewer dwellers to stay in shape.

2. Have students imitate some of the body movements of characters at the fair, for example, acrobats, stilt walkers, or jugglers.

3. Students may be interested in trying some orienteering activities. You should be able to locate several orienteering books at your local library or bookstore.

GRADE 5

DEAR MR. HENSHAW
Beverly Cleary
New York: Morrow, 1983

Summary:

Leigh Botts writes to his favorite book author. His letters are filled with questions and advice as well as a lot of revealing information about Leigh's life, his thoughts, and his feelings about his mother and father. This is a touching tale, told strictly through the correspondence of one boy, that offers a realistic and humorous look at the struggles of growing up. The book won the Newbery Award in 1984.

Critical Thinking Questions:

1. Why do you think Leigh wrote so many letters to a book author?

2. Why would he want to tell things about his family to a person he had never met?

3. What author would you like to correspond with? Why?

4. How is Leigh's life similar to or different from your life? Is Leigh someone you would like to know?

5. What kinds of questions would you like to ask Beverly Cleary, the author of the book?

Reading/Language Arts

1. Students will certainly enjoy reading other books by Beverly Cleary. Although there are many, here are a few to get them started: *Henry and Beezus* (New York: Morrow, 1952); *Mitch and Amy* (New York: Morrow, 1967); *Ramona the Pest* (New York: Morrow, 1968); and *Ramona Quimby, Age 8* (New York: Morrow, 1981).

2. Students should be encouraged to read about the life and writings of Beverly Cleary. Your school or local librarian will be able to supply several references. One particularly useful source is the author's own story: *A Girl from Yamhill* (New York: Morrow, 1988).

3. Have students put together a guidebook entitled "How to Become a Better Writer." Ask them to interview adults, teachers, businesspeople, reporters, and other children in the community on the tips and strategies that help people write. The information they collect can be assembled into a booklet to be distributed to other classes.

4. Students may enjoy setting up a pen pal network with students in another school. Contact colleagues in other schools or the education department of a local college and ask for the names of former students who have secured teaching positions in other parts of the state. Contact these individuals and invite their classes to correspond with the students in your class and vice versa. Encourage students to keep the letters flowing throughout the year (and beyond!).

5. Ask students to prepare a letter to Beverly Cleary commenting on this book or any other(s) she has written. Students may wish to include questions about the writing of children's books or about writing in general. Send the letter in care of Ms. Cleary's publisher (William Morrow and Co., 105 Madison Avenue, New York, NY 10016). Advise students that because she receives so much mail, they may not receive a personal reply, but there is certainly no harm in trying. (By the way, Beverly Cleary's birthday is April 12. Students may wish to send her a birthday card.)

Science/Health

1. Students may enjoy creating their own electronic gadgets, much like Leigh did. Various kits can be obtained at your local Radio Shack store. These include the "10 in One," "30 in One," and "50 in One" kits in the Science Fair line. For students interested in constructing their own burglar alarms, Natural Science Industries produces the "Electro-Tech Kit," available through science catalogs, which allows children to create a variety of electrical objects. Two useful books include *Experiments with Electric Currents*, by Harry Sootin (New York: Norton, 1969) and *Safe and Simple Electrical Experiments*, by Rudolf Graf (New York: Dover, 1973).

2. Students will certainly be interested in watching the development and growth of butterflies. Nasco (901 Janesville Avenue, Fort Atkinson, WI 53538; 800-558-9595) produces a "Butterfly Garden," which can be ordered through their catalog or found in many toy and hobby stores. Students will be able to observe and record the growth of butterflies from cocoons to adults.

Art

1. Have students put together an oversize collage of trucks and the trucking industry. Using pictures from old magazines as well as information and brochures collected from local trucking firms, students can assemble an informative collage for posting in the classroom or a wall of the school.

Math

1. Have students compute the number of miles from Leigh's home in Pacific Grove, California, to some of the other cities mentioned in the book (e.g., Bakersfield, CA; Taft, CA; Albuquerque, NM; Hermiston, OR). Later, have students figure out the number of miles between each of those cities and their school. These figures can be posted on a large classroom map of the United States.

2. Have students contact local trucking firms and ask for the number of miles (or number of hours) their drivers are allowed to cover within a twenty-four-hour period. With that data, have students figure out all the cities that can be reached from their town if a driver were to stay within the designated parameters. What towns could Leah's father drive to (from Pacific Grove, CA) with the time and distance restrictions?

Music

1. Have students check the record sections of their local library or college library for recordings of songs dealing with trucks or truck drivers (country/western songs might be a logical place to begin). Have students put together a listing or series of recordings of trucking songs to share with classmates. What is distinctive about these songs?

Social Studies

1. Students may be interested in obtaining travel and tourist information about California. They can write to the Office of Tourism, Box 189, Sacramento, CA 95812-0189. When material arrives, they should arrange it into an attractive display.

2. Students may be interested in putting together a large mural on the history of transportation in this country. Several teams of students could each work in completing the necessary research for one aspect of transportation (land, air, sea travel). Information, pictures, brochures, photographs, and the like can all be posted on the mural, which can be displayed in the school library.

3. Invite a social worker or psychologist to your classroom to talk about the nature of divorce (please be sensitive to the experiences of your students). The visitor can explain some of the statistics about divorce in this country and discuss the implications for family members. How to deal with divorce and its ramifications can also be part of the presentation. Students should be encouraged to ask questions.

Physical Education

1. Have students put together a series of activities or exercises that would be appropriate for truck drivers. Students may wish to interview truck drivers to find out what parts of their bodies they use most and how they maintain some degree of physical conditioning. Are there exercises (isometric) that can be done while driving? Are there activities that can be practiced while not on the road? Students should keep in mind that both men and women are truck drivers and need to maintain appropriate physical conditioning.

EATING ICE CREAM WITH A WEREWOLF
Phyllis Green
New York: Harper and Row, 1983

Summary:

Brad's mother and father are going away for a week and he and his little sister are left with Phoebe Hadley, the strangest baby-sitter of them all. With her book of spells, Phoebe conjures up weird events and mind-bending occurrences. Brad does not quite believe it all until he sees the delivery man. Nevertheless, this story is filled with giggles and guffaws and a host of delightful illustrations.

Critical Thinking Questions:

1. Would you like to be one of Brad's friends? What do you like most about him? What do you like least?

2. How are Brad's mother and father like your parents? How are they different? Would you want to have them as parents?

3. What are some things you enjoy doing on the weekend with your brothers and sisters? What are some things you like to do with your friends?

4. What kinds of things would you do if your parents were away for an entire week?

5. Do you know anyone like Phoebe? Would you want to know anyone like Phoebe? Why?

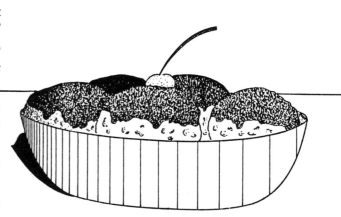

Reading/Language Arts

1. Have students assemble a list of books that would be appropriate to read aloud to a two-year-old child. Check with the school's librarian or the children's librarian at the local public library for recommendations. Have them collect an extensive list of books for duplication and sharing with families in local day care and preschool centers.

2. Students can be divided into small groups, each of which will prepare a definitive guide on "How to Train Your Baby-sitter." Using a light and humorous touch, students should be encouraged to provide fellow classmates with some tips and pointers on how baby-sitters should be trained, that is, ideas on how to get them to let kids do whatever they want, whenever they want. Of course, they will want to disseminate the final product to other classes.

3. Have students work in pairs to create sets of incantations or magic spells. Have them refer to the ones in the book as examples, then begin creating their own, with the emphasis on humor. These can be designed in several categories, as they were in *Dr. Curmudgeon's Book of Magic*, and posted on an appropriately designed bulletin board.

4. Have students check out several books on magic from the school or local public library. Discuss with them some of the similarities and differences in the books. Invite students to establish an attractive reading center in the classroom to get others to read the books. Of course, students should also be encouraged to put on a class magic show.

Science/Health

1. Students may be interested in growing their own mushrooms (the edible kinds). A "Mushroom-Farm-in-a-Box" can be obtained from Nasco (901 Janesville Road, Fort Atkinson, WI 53538; 800-558-9595); this kit provides students with everything they need to grow several crops of mushrooms over a three-month period.

2. Brad was interested in electricity and your students may be, too. Here are several books that will provide them with basic information as well as opportunities to construct some electrical projects: *Discovering Electricity*, by Neil Ardley (New York: Watts, 1984); *A Book About Electricity*, by Harlan Wade (Milwaukee, WI: Raintree, 1977); *Safe and Simple Electrical Experiments*, by Rudolf Graf (New York: Dover, 1973); and *How to Be an Inventor*, by Harvey Weiss (New York: Crowell, 1980).

3. Have students put together bulletin-board displays of the various types of birds mentioned in the story. Chickens, turkeys, and storks would all be suitable subjects for library investigation. Invite an ornithologist from a local college to share some data and information on birds with the class. One or more students may be interested in putting together a descriptive brochure on the marabou stork to be shared with other members of the class.

Art

1. Have small student groups each make a decorative sign for Phoebe's flower shop, "Fortunes and Fernery." Since she does not tell fortunes any more, how should the sign be designed to emphasize the "fernery" part of her business and play down the "fortune" part of the business?

2. Have students work in groups to design their own labels for ice cream. If students were approached to design a label for a new brand or new flavor of ice cream, what would it look like and how could it be made attractive to potential buyers?

Math

1. In the book, piano lessons were being offered at $8.00 for one-half hour of instruction. Have students design their own word problems for a series of piano lessons. For example, how much would it cost per month if Brad had one half-hour lesson every five days? If the parents only have $124 to spend on piano lessons, how many hours of instruction does that buy?

2. Have students check in local stores and ice cream parlors for the various prices of a quart of ice cream. Have them develop their data in the form of a chart or graph depicting the different flavors of ice cream and the establishments where ice cream is sold. What flavor costs the most? What establishment charges the most for ice cream? Where should students go and what flavor should they buy to be the most economical?

3. Have students look up the wing spans of different varieties of birds. Have students convert this information into bar graphs for posting in the classroom (the graphs can be organized into "Birds of North America," "Birds of Europe," or "Birds of South America).

Music

1. Have students assemble their own songbook about birds. Songs with the names of birds in the title (e.g., "When the Red, Red Robin Comes Bob, Bob, Bobbin' Along") or songs about one or more bird activities (e.g., "Come Fly with Me") could all be included in the songbook. Students should be encouraged to collect traditional as well as popular music.

Social Studies

1. The story took place in Madison, Wisconsin. Have students plot the distance from Madison to their home-town on a map of the United States. Have students also plot the distances from Madison to each of the towns or cities they have lived in during their lives. These distances can be indicated on the map with push pins and lengths of yarn.

2. Have students write to the Wisconsin Division of Tourism (Box 7606, Madison, WI 53707) to obtain descriptive brochures and information about that state. Students may also wish to write to the other states mentioned in the book. For example:

   Pennsylvania Department of Commerce, Bureau of Travel Development, 453 Forum Building, Harris-burg, PA 17120;

   Delaware Tourism Office, 99 Kings Highway, Dover, DE 19903;

   California Office of Tourism, Box 189, Sacramento, CA 95812;

   Idaho Travel Council, 700 West State Street, Boise, ID 83720.

3. Have students design their own replica of a native American village. Challenge them to design a model made entirely of clay as Brad and his friend Martin tried to do. Students will need to consult some library resources or their social studies text for various examples of villages.

4. Have students look into the history of the U.S. Postal Service. They may wish to interview local postal officials or obtain information from the U.S. Postal Service in Washington, DC. A book to get them started is *Special Delivery*, by Betty Brandt (Minneapolis, MN: Carolrhoda, 1988).

Physical Education

1. Have students set up a jogging course around the school grounds. In fact, students may wish to set up more than one course for individuals of varying athletic abilities. Have students use the course(s) periodically and attempt to lower their times for completing each course.

EINSTEIN ANDERSON SHOCKS HIS FRIENDS
Seymour Simon
New York: Puffin Books, 1986

Summary:

Adam Anderson got the nickname "Einstein" because he can solve any kind of problem, especially if it has something to do with science. Einstein Anderson uses his vast knowledge of electricity, biology, space science, and chemistry to solve a host of problems. He is also able to help his friends and protect others from bullies. This is one of a series of Einstein Anderson books that offer readers a painless way to read about science in action.

Critical Thinking Questions:

1. How do you think Einstein Anderson got to be so smart? Was he born that way or did he have to work at it? Why?

2. Would you enjoy having Einstein Anderson as a friend or a brother? Why?

3. If you were able to see in the dark, like a cat, how would this help you? What kinds of things would you be able to do better or differently?

4. If you could have any kind of animal as a pet, what would it be? What characteristics does that animal have that other animals do not have?

5. How do you feel about a barter system? Is is better than a system based on the exchange of money? Why do you think so?

Reading/Language Arts

1. Students will want to read this author's other Einstein Anderson books, including *Einstein Anderson Makes Up for Lost Time* (New York: Puffin Books, 1986) and *Einstein Anderson Lights Up the Sky* (New York: Bantam Books, 1984).

2. Challenge students to take a recently presented lesson in the science text and develop it into an Einstein Anderson story, although they may want to use their own name(s). They will benefit from working in small groups. This activity can take place over the course of the entire year and can be an incentive for students to combine reading, writing, and science into a single exciting activity.

3. Select several stories from the book and read the titles and the first part of each tale to your students. Have students work in small groups to make predictions on what they think each story will be about. What scientific principles do they think will be covered in each story? How do they think Einstein will solve each case?

4. Have students keep a mystery journal for a week. Invite them to list some of the "mysteries" that occur in class (e.g., a missing book, lost lunch money, a student is absent, etc.). Have students share their mysteries at the end of the week. In small groups, ask students to list all the steps they would follow to try to solve each mystery. Do they note any similarities in the steps? Does this suggest that there may be a universal way of approaching problem solving? Students may then wish to make up their own guidebook to problem solving.

Science/Health

1. Students may be interested in solving science problems on a daily basis. A good source for this once-a-day activity is *Think About It! Science Problems of the Day*, by Anthony D. Fredericks (Sunnyvale, CA: Creative Publications, 1988). This teacher resource lists over 200 daily thought-provoking experiences designed to stimulate curiosity, interest, and problem-solving skills in science.

2. Have students set up eye experiments that test the time it takes students' eyes to dilate or constrict. Students can all be in a darkened room for a length of time, then shine a flashlight in each other's eyes and time the dilation. The experiment can be reversed in order to measure the average length of time for students' pupils to constrict. The various times can be averaged and recorded on a large class chart. Have students speculate on any significant differences or similarities.

3. Students may wish to conduct plant experiments to test Einstein's theory of plant growth. Have students obtain several identical house plants. Place one on a windowsill, cover the soil of another with a plastic lid and hang it upside down from the ceiling near the window, and place another in the center of the classroom. Have students notice the direction of plant growth in all three samples. What can they conclude about plant growth and sunlight?

4. Have students place new coins of varying denominations on a windowsill outside the classroom. Have them record the length of time it takes each one to tarnish (some will not). What can students surmise about the materials used to make the different denominations of coins and their rate of tarnishing? Would those conclusions hold true with other objects made from the same material(s)? Have students test their theories with other metal objects.

Art

1. Invite students to invent or create their own form of hieroglyphics, just as Margaret did in the story. What symbols would they want to use and what significance would each symbol or combination of symbols hold?

Math

1. Fill three jars of different sizes full of pennies. Invite students to predict the number of pennies in each jar. Have students discuss the nature of estimation and its usefulness in everyday life. Why do we not always need to know the exact amount or quantity of an object or objects? In what kinds of situations would estimation be useful? In what situations would it be detrimental? Afterward, have students count the number of pennies in each jar and compare the totals with their estimates.

2. Have students convert U.S. currency into the currency of various countries (e.g., pesos, francs, kroner, pounds, etc.). Check with a local bank to obtain current exchange rates. Then have students calculate the answers to previously completed word problems (those dealing with money) in terms of the currency of one or more countries.

Music

1. Students are sometimes surprised to learn that music and sound are the products of some very interesting scientific principles. Students should be encouraged to investigate the nature of music via library resources. One book that will help them tremendously is *The Magic of Sound*, by Anthony Kramer (New York: Morrow, 1982). You may with to contact a musicologist or physics instructor from a nearby college to visit your class and give a simple demonstration on creating sound, particularly music.

Social Studies

1. Invite a local archaeologist to your classroom to explain the nature of that occupation (contact a local college or museum of natural history). Have students ask about some recent discoveries made around the world that give us insight into our ancestors and their lifestyles. What has been the most meaningful archaeological discovery in the last fifty years?

2. Ask students to investigate barter systems from around the world. What type of system was used by native Americans, in Middle Eastern countries, or in primitive societies? What similarities do these systems have? What differences? Have students present their collected data in the form of an oral or written report.

Physical Education

1. Discuss with students the reactions neutrons, protons, and electrons have in relation to each other. With that data in mind, challenge students to invent some physical activities that would demonstrate those attractions and reactions, for example, a form of square dancing, a parachute game in which several different colored balls are placed on a parachute held by many students, or some sort of relay race. Invite students to invent a variety of "physical" models.

THE GREEN BOOK
Jill Paton Walsh
New York: Farrar, Straus & Giroux, 1982

Summary:

Pattie and her family are among the last to escape from the dying planet Earth. While the grown-ups build houses and plant crops, Pattie and her friends do some exploring and find trees filled with sugar and moth people. The existence of the colony is threatened when the crops fail and their supplies run low. Pattie and her sister take a chance that might let them all survive.

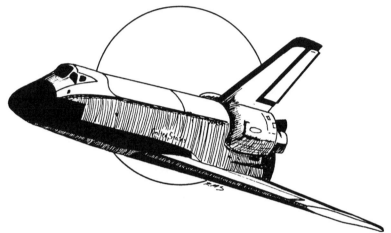

Critical Thinking Questions:

1. What do you think was the disaster on Earth that forced everyone to leave?

2. If you had to leave the planet Earth, what supplies would you want to take along with you?

3. What do you think you would miss the most about life on Earth?

4. If you could take only one book to a distant planet, what book would you wish to take? Why?

5. Why would keeping a diary be important for someone living on a distant planet?

Reading/Language Arts

1. Have each student prepare a "Green Book" diary. Suggestions for diary entries include one or more of the following: a) write about the book as it is being read; b) write as if you were going to a new planet; c) write a diary about your feelings during various stages of the journey.

2. Students may enjoy reading other books about space and space travel. These can include: *A Wrinkle in Time*, by Madeleine L'Engle (New York: Farrar, Straus & Giroux, 1962); *The Wonderful Flight to the Mushroom Planet*, by Eleanor Cameron (Boston: Little, Brown, 1954); and *Born to Light*, by Paul Jacobs (New York: Scholastic, 1988).

3. Students may also enjoy reading other books by Jill Paton Walsh, including *Gaffer Samson's Luck* (New York: Farrar, Straus & Giroux, 1984); *Goldenglove* (New York: Farrar, Straus & Giroux, 1972); and *Unleaving* (New York: Farrar, Straus & Giroux, 1976).

4. Have students make a paper quilt of the story. Cut a piece of butcher paper 3 by 6 feet for the backing. Give students several 10-inch squares of white paper. Ask each student to draw an illustration, write poetry, record favorite character sayings, or the like on each square. Paste the squares on the butcher paper in even rows and columns with equal areas of the backing as borders around each square. Hang the entire quilt on a classroom wall.

5. One of the books the children had on the new planet was *Robinson Crusoe.* You may elect to do one of the following activities: a) read portions of *Robinson Crusoe* to students on a daily basis; b) have students make regular diary entries as though they were stranded alone on a desert island; and c) have students make lists of the things they would take to a desert island and things they would take to a distant planet. How are the lists similar? How are the lists different?

Science/Health

1. Have each student plant a small garden. Obtain several egg cartons and place some potting soil in the bottom of each compartment. Carefully plant some vegetable seeds in each compartment and water lightly. Water the compartments every other day or so just to keep them moist. After a few days, some plants will begin to sprout. Students may wish to track their miniature gardens by planting many different varieties of seeds in the egg cartons and recording the growth patterns of the various plants.

2. Students may be interested in growing butterflies in the classroom. A "Butterfly Garden Kit" (no. 512-1230H) is available through Holcomb's Educational Materials (3205 Harvard Avenue, Cleveland, OH 44105). The kit includes a butterfly house, guidebook, accessories, and a coupon for a supply of caterpillars. The kit allows students to watch the butterfly life cycle as caterpillars feed, grow, spin their cocoons, and emerge as Painted Lady butterflies.

3. Invite a volunteer from the local chapter of the American Red Cross to visit your class to explain the contents of an emergency first aid kit. What materials and supplies should be kept in a standard kit? How should each of the items be used? Where should the kits be stored so that they are easily accessible?

4. Students may wish to experiment with hydroponic (soilless) growth. Have students float several sponges in a large flat container of water. Sprinkle the top of each sponge with grass seed and place the containers in sunlight. Have students check the sponges every few days to see if the seeds sprout. Students may wish to experiment with other plant varieties to determine which ones are best suited to hydroponic conditions. You may also wish to obtain the "Hydroponics Nursery Unit" from Carolina Biological Supply Company (2700 York Road, Burlington, NC 27215; 919-584-0381 [catalog no. 66-6860]).

5. Have students read and research *50 Simple Things Kids Can Do to Save the Earth*, by Earthworks Group (Kansas City, MO: Andrews and McMeel, 1990). Ask them to make a list of the ten most serious environmental problems facing the planet today. Have students design and develop plans for dealing with each of those problems. Encourage lots of class discussion and debate.

Art

1. Have students remove their shoes and socks. Ask each one to step into a flat pan of tempera paint mixed with a little dish detergent (for easier cleanup). Have each child step onto a large sheet of paper with their feet crossed (the left foot is on the right side; the right foot is on the left side) or one foot at a time. Have them step off the paper and clean up feet. Then add a head, antennae, and background scenery to each of their "butterflies."

2. Have students make shoebox dioramas of the new planet. Students can gather small plants, twigs, leaves, and other natural substances during a nature walk around the school. Combine these materials to create all-natural dioramas for display in the classroom.

Math

1. Have students check various science books, including *The Planets in our Solar System*, by Franklyn Branley (New York: Crowell, 1981); *Nova Space Explorer's Guide: Where to Go and What to See*, by Richard Maurer (New York: Potter, 1985); and *National Geographic Picture Atlas of our Universe*, by Roy Gallant (Washington, DC: National Geographic Society, 1986). Have them make comparative charts of the distances of each planet from the sun, from the Earth, and from each other.

2. The trip for those in the book took four years. Have students calculate how old everybody in their family would be if they took the trip. You may wish to challenge some students to calculate how far away the planet was if the spaceship traveled at an average speed of 25,000 mph.

3. Students may wish to create their own shadow clocks. Fill a coffee can with sand and place a two-foot dowel in the center. Put the can in a sunny location on the playground early in the morning. Have students put a stone at the top of the stick's shadow at 9:00 a.m. An hour later (10:00 a.m.), have students place another stone at the top of the dowel's shadow. Continue this process for the rest of the school day. Students can check the next day to see if the stone placements are still accurate. Chalk dots on the playground for each hour. Have students check their timepiece periodically throughout the year to see if there are any changes. How can they account for those changes?

Music

1. Have students learn the song "Bringing in the Sheaves" from *Family Songbook*, music arranged and edited by Dan Fox (New York: Henry Holt & Co., 1987). Have students create movements to go along with the song or discuss why this tune would be an appropriate accompaniment for this book.

2. Play some classical musical selections (for example, Chopin's Piano Scherzos 1 and 2) and encourage students to create and invent movements for a "Dance of the Moth."

Social Studies

1. Have students research one or more early explorers (Columbus, de Gama, Balboa, Magellan, etc.). Ask them to explain the similarities between those early explorers and Pattie and her family. How is space exploration similar to sea or land exploration?

2. Have students choose two favorite explorers, one early explorer and one space explorer. Direct students to design commemorative stamps for each of those explorers on large sheets of construction paper. The stamps can be posted around the room with accompanying captions and relevant information.

3. Have students work in small groups to discuss what they think is important for each of the following to survive: family (food, shelter, etc.); community (laws, transportation, etc.); city (police, sanitation, etc.); county; state; nation; and world. Have students erect large charts with lists of the essentials needed by each of these groups.

4. Contact your local chapter of the American Red Cross and ask for a copy of the *Family Survival Guide*. Discuss the instructions and preparations necessary for surviving a catastrophic event such as a hurricane or tornado. Invite a Red Cross volunteer to explain to students the emergency plans for your local community and how students can help ensure that the plans are carried out in the event of an emergency.

5. Have students decide on ten or fifteen items that would be representative of their class to be placed in a time capsule. Put the selected items in a box and have it placed in the school district's safe (usually located in the business office). Retrieve the box at the end of the year and ask students to discuss whether the items were and still are representative of who they were months ago. If they had to do it all over again, what different items would be placed in the box? What items would be left out?

Physical Education

1. Have students play the games that the children in the book remembered, including "Hopscotch" and "Ring Around the Rosey." Have students invent variations of these games for older or younger children.

2. Students can invent their own relay races in which teams of students run back and forth between different "planets" drawn on the playground. A "cocoon" can be passed back and forth between team members. The team to arrive first at the final planet is declared the winner.

MORE SCARY STORIES TO TELL IN THE DARK
Alvin Schwartz
New York: Harper and Row, 1984

Summary:

People who take the form of cats, hands dangling inside the closet, strange disappearances and reappearances, corpses, goblins, and ghosts all haunt this collection of scary stories and frightful tales. The emphasis is on fright and the stories retold in this book offer young readers a potpourri of possible campfire, slumber party, and after-class tales to share and enjoy.

Critical Thinking Questions:

1. Which of the stories was the scariest? What made it so scary?

2. What elements does a scary story have to have?

3. Do you know any stories that are scarier than the stories in this book? Can you share one with us?

4. Which one of these stories do you think would make a good movie? Why?

5. Could any event in your life be included in a collection of scary stories? Can you describe it?

Reading/Language Arts

1. Students will enjoy reading other scary and ghost stories. Introduce them to books such as *Famous Ghost Stories*, by Bennett Cerf (New York: Random House, 1944); *Things That Go Bump in the Night*, by Louis Jones (New York: Hill and Wang, 1959); *The Thing at the Foot of the Bed and Other Scary Stories*, by Maria Leach (New York: World Publishing, 1959); and *Scary Stories to Tell in the Dark*, by Alvin Schwartz (New York: Lippincott, 1981).

2. Have students write a letter to one of the characters in the book. Which character would they choose, a protagonist or a victim? Why was that particular individual chosen?

3. Have students work in small groups to rewrite one of the stories in the book to include the names of classmates and locations in their community. Provide opportunities for students to share their stories in written or oral form.

4. Assemble a group of six to eight students. Ask one student to begin telling a scary story and get as far as possible in three minutes. At the end of the three minutes, the story is continued by the next person, who also has three minutes. The process continues until everyone has had a chance to contribute to the story, with the last person devising an appropriate ending (scary, of course).

Science/Health

1. Many scary stories rely on the reader's knowledge of the human anatomy. Invite a professor from a local college or the school nurse to give your students a quick lesson on human anatomy, with particular reference to hands,

brains, hearts, and the other body parts that tend to appear most in scary stories. An excellent supplemental film (which has won many awards) is *Man: The Incredible Machine* (Washington, DC: National Geographic Society, 1975 [catalog no. 51255]).

2. Students may be interested in creating a small sample of fog. Obtain a large-mouth jar and a margarine container. Fill the jar half-full with very warm water. Put the margarine container in the mouth of the jar (the joint may need to be sealed with paraffin or petroleum jelly). Fill the margarine container with ice cubes. Have students observe what happens inside the jar. Depending on the room temperature of the classroom, either a small cloud, some fog, or lots of water droplets will form inside the jar. Students should experiment with different water temperatures and room temperatures to create the best conditions for manufacturing fog.

3. Cats are a popular animal in scary stories. Have students conduct some research on the behavior and characteristics of cats. They may assemble their data into a descriptive scrapbook for classroom display.

4. Students may wish to construct their own models of a human skeleton. One version, a scientifically accurate skeleton assembled from die-cut cardboard sheets, is available from Albion Import Export Company (Coolidge Bank Building, 65 Main Street, Watertown, MA 02172). Another version, slightly less expensive, is produced by Lindberg and can be found in most toy and hobby stores.

Art

1. Have students put together a collage of a haunted house. Using pictures from old magazines and a large sheet of construction paper, students can build a haunted house to their own specifications.

Math

1. The story "The Bad News" dealt with baseball. Have students compute the batting averages of some of their favorite baseball players. The statistics are printed in most daily newspapers, including times at bat and number of hits. With those two figures, students can compute batting averages and check them against the figures reported in the newspaper.

2. In "Wonderful Sausage," various individuals are turned into sausage. Have students research the prices of various types of sausage in their local community and prepare a comparative chart listing all the prices and varieties available. Have students compute prices for various weights (such as the equivalent weights of classmates) of sausage at various stores.

3. Most scary stories take place at night. Have students compute and chart the length of the night, from the exact time of sunset to the exact time of sunrise, at various times during the year. Figures can be converted into hours, minutes, and seconds.

Music

1. Have students check with the music teacher or with their friends to obtain various sound-effects records. Have them put together a recording of sounds and songs appropriate for one or more stories in this book.

Social Studies

1. Students may be interested in the history of ghost stories or in scary tales from other countries. Have them conduct some library research and make a presentation on the stories that we tell in this country as well as stories that are popular in other countries. Some books to get them started include *Haunted England: A Survey of*

English Ghostlore, by Christina Hole (London: B. T. Batsford, 1950); and *Legends of the City of Mexico*, by Thomas Janvier (New York: Harper, 1910).

2. Invite students to write a biographical sketch of a ghost. Introduce students to biographies of famous people and the chronology of events that are reported in those stories. Have students create their own biographies of scary creatures, whether real or imagined.

3. Ask students to investigate the Salem Witch Trials and the controversy surrounding that period of American history. Ask students to prepare a brochure on the witch trials for sharing with other classes.

4. Contact a local or regional folklore society in your area and invite one of their storytellers to visit your classroom to share some tales. Have the individual share some of the history behind the stories told as well as data on their origins.

Physical Education

1. Have students conduct races without using some parts of their anatomy. For example, have students race a course with their hands tied behind their backs or without using their legs (use scooters if they are available from the P.E. teacher). Have students conduct blindfold races where they cannot use their eyes (use extreme caution). Challenge students to invent other types of races in which one or more body parts cannot be used.

NOTHING'S FAIR IN FIFTH GRADE
Barthe DeClements
New York: Scholastic, 1981

Summary:

Things begin to happen when the new student, Elsie Edwards, is assigned to Jenifer's fifth-grade class. Not only is Elsie fat, but she is also accused of stealing everyone's lunch money. But that is not Jenny's only problem — she is also failing math. Little does she know that Elsie will be her saving grace, in more ways than one.

Critical Thinking Questions:

1. Would you want to have Elsie as a friend? Would she have been more likely to have been your friend before the story started or at the end of the story? Explain.

2. What type of person is Jenifer? Is she someone you would want to have in your class?

3. Would you want to be a member of Jenny's class? Why or why not?

4. What was your most embarrassing moment in school?

5. After reading this book, would you want to be a teacher? What do you think would be your greatest challenge as a teacher? What would you do about it?

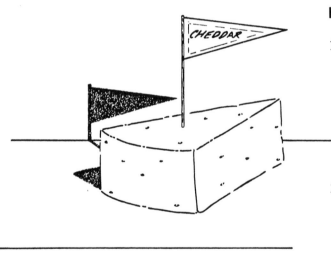

Reading/Language Arts

1. Provide an opportunity for your students to establish a tutoring service for students in lower grades. Ask students to list the skills and talents they would be willing to share with another student (the skills do not necessarily have to be academic). Establish some times, dates, and places for students to tutor others on a one-to-one basis. Have tutors maintain diaries of their experiences to share back in class.

2. Have students create a daily diary written from the viewpoint of a severely overweight person (be sensitive to those students who are overweight). What kinds of experiences would they encounter on a daily basis? How would they react? Provide a forum in which students can discuss and share their diaries.

3. Have students read other books about overweight children. How do those books compare with this one? What similarities are there in the personalities of the overweight individuals? Excellent books to start with are *Blubber*, by Judy Blume (New York: Bradbury, 1974) or *Jelly Belly*, by Robert Kimmel Smith (New York: Delacorte, 1981).

4. Have small groups of students interview the principal or other administrators in the school district on their interpretations of bad behavior. What constitutes bad behavior on the part of students? How are students expected to behave in the classroom? In the hallways? In the cafeteria? On the school grounds? What kinds of punishment are

meted out to misbehaving students? Have students write their own discipline policy. Ask them to compare theirs to the school's actual policy.

5. Students will also enjoy reading another book by this author: *Sixth Grade Can Really Kill You* (New York: Viking, 1985).

Science/Health

1. Invite a dietitian or nutritionist to visit your classroom and present information on the eating habits of fifth-grade students. What kinds of food should students be eating to maintain proper body weight? What are some of the dangers of being overweight? What causes it? How can it be prevented?

2. Have each student make a list of all the foods they eat in a twenty-four-hour period. Provide students with calorie charts and ask them to compute the number of calories they consumed during the twenty-four hours (this can also be done as a math activity). Have students compare their calorie consumption with the recommended daily allowance for an individual of their body type, age, and physical activity.

3. Students in the book had to put together a skit about first aid. Have your students do the same. What events or materials should be part of the skit? What message do the players wish to get across to the audience? What lessons are there to learn?

4. An outstanding sound filmstrip to share with your students is *What's Good To Eat: Foods the Body Needs* (Washington, DC: National Geographic Society, 1980 [catalog no. 04188]). This filmstrip presents information on the importance of eating well-balanced meals and the role of nutrients in supplying energy for the body.

Art

1. Ask students to assemble portraits of each of the major characters. Some students can stand between a strong light source and a sheet of paper. Other students can trace the silhouettes of students and turn them into character portraits. A "Rogue's Gallery" of book characters can be displayed on one wall of the classroom.

2. Have students contact a local law enforcement agency and obtain information on the dangers of hitchhiking. Have students use their information to create a persuasive poster or series of posters to be displayed around the school.

Math

1. Challenge students to create an appropriate math test for students in a grade lower than their own. Have the students interview a teacher at that grade level to determine the math objectives being covered. Then have students design a test that they could administer and score.

2. Have students interview students in the high school, particularly those in advanced math classes. Have students inquire about some of the tricks of the trade used to solve complex math problems. How does one get to be proficient in math? What techniques or strategies are helpful in solving certain kinds of math problems? Students may want to present their findings in the form of a descriptive brochure.

3. Contact the education department of a local college and invite the professor who teaches the elementary math methods courses to make a presentation to your class. What tips or techniques can that individual offer that would be useful to your students in solving the math problems currently being tackled? The professor may be willing to bring some college students to help demonstrate various strategies.

Music

1. The students in the book were scheduled to have a school dance. Have the students in your class put together the musical selections for an imaginary school dance. What songs or artists would they want to feature? Would they want a variety of music, or just one kind? What musical selections should be played to ensure the success of the dance? Be sure to have students defend their selections.

Social Studies

1. Ask your students to conduct interviews of other students in the school on the nature and causes of stealing. Why do people steal? What is gained by stealing? What is lost? Have students compile their data into a brochure for distribution throughout the school.

2. Have students work in small groups to design and develop a classroom "bill of rights." What rights should students have? How should teachers behave toward students? How should students behave toward teachers? What guarantees should students have? Students may wish to compare their bill of rights with the Bill of Rights to the U.S. Constitution.

Physical Education

1. Have students put together a booklet of games and activities that can be played during recess time. Encourage students to interview students and teachers in other schools to gather ideas for physical activities that can be completed in relatively short periods of time (recesses).

2. Students may enjoy a simple session of square dancing, as the students in the book had to do. Your music teacher or P.E. teacher should be able to provide you with instructions and some musical selections.

OWLS IN THE FAMILY
Farley Mowat
New York: Bantam Books, 1981

Summary:

This book tells of the adventures (or misadventures) of two owls from Saskatchewan, Wol and Weeps, who shake up an entire neighborhood, turn a house topsy-turvy, and outsmart the family dog. Wol is a wonderful bird who brings dead skunks to the family dinner table and terrorizes the minister, the postman, and the French teacher. Weeps, who never learns to fly, is a comical bird and is afraid of everything except the dog.

Critical Thinking Questions:

1. Which of the animals in this story would you choose as a pet? Why?

2. What do you think the maid, the minister, and the teacher told other people about Wol?

3. Why do you think Billy's dad allowed him to keep the owls when he had so many other pets?

4. What kinds of adventures would the owls have if you were to bring them to your house? How would your parents feel about having owls as pets?

5. What do you feel was the most humorous incident in this story? Is that incident similar to anything that has happened to you?

Reading/Language Arts

1. Students will enjoy reading another book by Farley Mowat: *Lost in the Barrens* (New York: McClelland and Stewart, 1966, 1984).

2. Challenge students to rewrite portions of the story from the owls' point of view. Did the owls consider themselves to be as bad as everyone made them out to be?

3. The owls in the story had no parents to teach them how to fly. Ask students to create lists of the things their parents have taught them. Generate a class discussion about things on students' lists that they would eventually have learned on their own versus things that must be learned from a parent or older adult.

4. Billy had to find a good home for the owls. Have students work in small groups of two or three to develop one or more classified advertisements for the owls. Provide groups with examples from the local newspaper. Collect all the ads in a newspaper format and post in the classroom.

Science/Health

1. Over twenty animals are mentioned in the story. Have students work in small groups to research selected animals and make a presentation to the rest of the class. Whenever possible, encourage students to bring an example or two of their selected animal(s) for "Show and Tell."

2. An excellent series of sound filmstrips produced by the National Geographic Society is The Life of Animals (1976 [catalog no. 03781]). The five filmstrips in the series cover ways animals get food, animal homes, how animals move, how they protect themselves, and animals and their families.

3. Take students for a nature walk near the school or out in the local community. Challenge students to look for—without disturbing!—various types of bird nests. If this is not possible, visit a nearby museum of natural history or set up a presentation by an ornithologist from a local college.

4. Animals use many different types of defense mechanisms, such as teeth, claws, horns, antlers, spines, scent, stinging, etc. Invite student groups to create lists of various defense mechanisms and the animals that use them. The list can be posted in the classroom and added to over a period of time.

5. Divide a box of toothpicks into two piles. Paint the toothpicks in one pile green and the toothpicks in another pile brown. Randomly scatter all the toothpicks over a section of grass. Provide students with tweezers or barbecue tongs and ask them to pick up as many toothpicks as they can. Later discuss with them the color that was easier to locate and pick up. Also, discuss protective coloration and how animals use it as a form of protection from and defense against their enemies.

Art

1. Bring a large tree branch into your classroom and anchor it in a bucket filled with sand. Have students create models of owls from toilet tissue tubes, brown construction paper, pile cleaners, glue, and markers. When the models are complete, perch them in the tree branch.

2. Have students bring several shoeboxes to the classroom. Challenge students to create several versions of circus wagons as the boys did to use in the pet parade.

Math

1. Have students research the wingspans of different birds, including owls. Have them make a comparative chart of wingspans from the smallest (the Helena hummingbird—3 inches) to the largest (the wandering albatross—10½ feet).

2. The boys' pet rats kept reproducing. Provide students problems such as the following: If a pair of mice had two offspring each month, how many offspring would they have in a year? If each of those offspring had two offspring per month, how many mice would there be in two years? What if each pair of mice had three offspring every three weeks? Also discuss why, if so many mice have so many offspring, is the planet not covered with mice?

3. Have students arrange the animals in the book into various sets. These sets could include *feathers, fur, scales, living, non-living, were alive,* and *never alive,* for example. Have students arrange the sets into different configurations via Venn diagrams.

Music

1. Obtain a copy of the Canadian national anthem and play it for the students. Ask them to discuss similarities and differences between that anthem and the "Star-Spangled Banner."

Social Studies

1. Have students find Saskatchewan on a map of North America. Have them measure the distances from various cities in Saskatchewan and their town. Later, students may wish to obtain a road map of Canada and the United States and plot the fastest or most scenic route to one of the major cities from their town.

2. Saskatchewan is one of the prairie provinces. Encourage students to make a salt-dough map of a prairie for display in the classroom. Students may wish to place small figures, settlements, and bits of flora on their prairies.

3. The people of Canada speak one of two languages, English or French. For that reason, many of the products made in Canada have labels and directions printed in both languages. You may be able to obtain some items from your local grocery store that have been shipped from Canada and have both French and English labels. Have students bring in other examples of food that might be imported from Canada and provide their own French/English labels. Invite a language teacher from the high school to help you out.

4. Have students research the history of the Mounties, including how they started, what they do today, and the territory they cover. Student teams can put together an informative booklet listing various facts and fictions about this law enforcement group.

Physical Education

1. Invite students to invent a new game called "Prey and Predator." The game can have rules as simple as those for "Tag" or as complex as those for "Capture the Flag."

2. Have students play "Can the Can" (using a beach ball) as the boys did in the story.

THE RELUCTANT DRAGON
Kenneth Grahame
New York: Holiday, 1938

Summary:

This is a timeless tale of a young boy, a large creature, and their very special relationship. When the boy's father discovers a dragon, the boy and the dragon find they have many things to share. When Saint George comes to slay the dragon, the boy must devise a plan that is satisfactory to all.

Critical Thinking Questions:

1. If you were the mediator between Saint George and the dragon, what would you have done or said?

2. How might the story have been different if Saint George had not believed the boy?

3. Why do you think townspeople lied about the deeds of the dragon?

4. What career do you think the boy will choose when he is an adult? Why would that be an appropriate occupation for him?

5. What do you think becomes of the dragon? If you were the author of this story, what would you have the dragon do?

Reading/Language Arts

1. Students will probably enjoy reading other stories about dragons.

2. The dragon in the book loved poetry and would create his own. Students may want to write their own poetry, too, using events from the story or from their own lives. They may also enjoy listening to dragon poetry such as "The Gold Tinted Dragon" from *Dogs and Dragons, Trees and Dreams*, by Karla Kuskin (New York: Harper and Row, 1980).

3. Before reading the book, students may enjoy watching a video or movie about dragons. Two that may be available at your local library include *Dragon Tears* (New York: McGraw-Hill, 1962) and *The Reluctant Dragon* (Los Angeles: Buena Vista Home Entertainment [Walt Disney], 1950).

4. Have students list the characteristics of the dragon. Have them list the characteristics of a very mean dragon. Later, have students make up a guidebook on *Dragons: Their Personalities and Behavior*. Have students provide information in the guidebook that would help other individuals identify any dragon they may happen to meet, according to its personality.

Science/Health

1. The dragon mentioned that he went underground when "the earth sneezed or shook itself, or the bottom dropped." Have students research and discuss possible explanations for this phenomenon. Students may include earthquakes, landslides, or other natural geological occurrences.

2. Some people argue that the Komodo dragon is either a very large lizard or a small dragon. Whatever it is, it is certainly one of the most interesting creatures on Earth. Students may be interested in conducting some library research to find out as much as they can about this modern-day dragon. Have students make a descriptive poster listing all the data they can discover about this animal, including photographs, pictures, or illustrations.

3. Have students create several lists of all the animals that live in caves. Students may wish to prepare a list of mammals (bats and bears), reptiles (snakes), amphibians, birds, and fish that reside in caverns and caves. Their data can be combined and displayed on large wall murals.

4. Invite a geologist from a local college to visit and explain how caves are created, as well as describing some of the more famous caves in the country.

Art

1. Students may wish to create imaginary armor vests from paper grocery bags. A place for the head and both arms can be cut from the bottom and sides of a single bag. Each student should be encouraged to design a family crest to be displayed on the front of the suit of armor.

2. Students can create a large Chinese dragon from a cardboard box and an old sheet. The box (which is used as the head of the dragon) can be decorated with a variety of oriental designs. The sheet (under which three or four students will walk) can be designed and decorated to resemble a dragon. Students may wish to walk their dragon through the hallways of the school or suspend the dragon from the ceiling of the classroom.

Math

1. The size of the dragon in the book was equivalent to four carthorses. Have students research the various dimensions of common horses and estimate the approximate size of the dragon. A facsimile of the dragon can be drawn with chalk on the playground and colored with a variety of different chalks.

Music

1. Play some traditional English folk songs for students and ask them to discuss the implications of the words and the nature of the various melodies. Songs such as "Greensleeves," "Lavender's Blue," and "Scarborough Fair" would all be appropriate. A good resource is *Go In and Out the Window*, music arranged and edited by Dan Fox (New York: Henry Holt and Co., 1987).

Social Studies

1. Write to the nearest office of the British Tourist Authority and request information and brochures on travel in England. If there is no such office in a nearby large city, your students can write to the British Tourist Authority, 40 West 57th Street, New York, NY 10019. When material arrives have students set up an attractive display or center highlighting some of the attractions and sights in England.

2. Contact your county extension agent and ask for the name of a nearby sheep farmer. Invite that individual to share some information with your students on sheep farming. The person should be able to talk about how sheep are raised and cared for, some of the diseases of sheep, and the advantages of raising sheep as opposed to raising cattle.

3. The National Geographic Society (Washington, DC) has two filmstrips that will be of interest to your students. The first, *The Renaissance* (1983 [catalog no. 04595]) describes the events and ideas that guided the development of Renaissance history and culture. The second, *Geography of Europe Series—Part II, Western Europe* (1982 [catalog no. 04489]), describes England as well as France, the Netherlands, and Belgium.

Physical Education

1. Students may wish to play a game of "Dragons and Knights." Divide the class into two teams. Have the teams line up facing each other. One group are dragons, the other group are knights. When the caller (teacher) calls "dragons," the knights must run to the end zone (goal) before being tagged by one of the dragons. Knights who are tagged must go to the other team and become dragons. If the caller calls "knights," the dragons must run to their goal before being tagged. The game concludes after a specified period of time (for example, ten minutes). The side having the most players is declared the winner. The game can be made more complicated by calling "dragons" and "knights" at odd times throughout the course of action.

WHERE THE BUFFALOES BEGIN
Olaf Baker
New York: Warne, 1981

Summary:

Little Wolf, a courageous American Indian boy, longs to find the lake described in a legend of his people—the lake where the buffaloes begin. In his quest to fulfill that dream, he begins an adventure that ends with an unforgettable ride through the night to save his people.

Critical Thinking Questions:

1. Why do some people still perceive Native Americans to be bad people?

2. Would you have liked to live as a Native American in the 1800s? How would life then be different from your life now?

3. How do you think Little Wolf felt when he realized that his people were in danger? Have you ever been in a similar situation or had similar feelings?

4. Do you think Little Wolf should have been punished for leaving the camp without permission? Why?

5. What do you think was the most frightening thing Little Wolf faced? Did he react in the same way you would have reacted? Why or why not?

Reading/Language Arts

1. Discuss sign language as a means of communication. You may wish to teach students a few signs used by Plains Indians. Many such signs can be found in America's Fascinating Indian Heritage (Pleasantville, NY: Reader's Digest Association, 1978).

2. Ask students to create and write a character sketch of Little Wolf. What did he look like? What were some of his qualities?

3. Have students write a series of letters to Little Wolf. The letters can inquire about Native American life, tribal customs, and typical events in his life. The letters can be sent to students in other classes who have read the book and can answer in the voice of Little Wolf.

4. Students may enjoy reading other books about Native American life including one or more of the following: *Indians of the Northern Plains*, by William Powers (New York: Putnam, 1969); *Indians of the Southern Plains*, by William Powers (New York: Putnam, 1971); *Indians of the Southwest*, by Gordon Baldwin (New York: Putnam, 1970). Have students compare the lifestyles of various tribes. Students may wish to write about the influence of geography and climate on Native American life.

5. Divide the class into several small groups and instruct each group to create an alternate ending for the story. Have each group share their ending with the entire class and decide which ending is most exciting, most plausible, or most dramatic. Written endings should be posted on the bulletin board for sharing.

Science/Health

1. Invite a meteorologist from the local television station or college to visit your class to explain the nature of wind. What causes wind? How is it measured? How are different wind speeds classified? Students should be prepared to ask questions of the visitor. Background information can be obtained from books such as *The Usborne Book of Weather Facts*, by Anita Ganeri (Tulsa, OK: EDC Publishing, 1987); *Air, Light, and Water*, by Mary-Jane Wilkins (New York: Random House, 1990); and *Weather*, by Brian Cosgrove (New York: Knopf, 1991).

2. Have students compile a list of descriptive information about buffaloes. How important were buffaloes to the lives of the Plains Indians? How many uses did the Indians have for buffalo products? What was the life span of a buffalo? Information can be garnered from several sources, including *America's Fascinating Indian Heritage* (Pleasantville, NY: Reader's Digest Association, 1978) and *The Indian and the Buffalo*, by Robert Hofsinde (New York: Morrow, 1961).

3. Have students read *Corn Is Maize: The Gift of the Indians*, by Aliki (New York: Crowell, 1976). Afterward, obtain some packets of corn seed from a local garden center and allow students to grow their own corn plants according to directions on the seed packets. Fill paper cups with a mixture of potting soil and dirt and plant two or three seeds in each cup. Place the cups in a sunny location and water occasionally. If it is springtime, the seeds can be planted outdoors in an appropriate location. Provide opportunities for students to chart the growth of their corn plants.

Art

1. Check with a local craft store and obtain several bead kits for your students. Students can create examples of Native American belts and bracelets for display or individual wearing.

2. Provide students with finger paints and paper and have them create various paintings of buffaloes and buffalo hunts.

Math

1. Have students conduct some library research on the dimensions and weight of both the buffalo and an average-size horse. Have students develop a comparative chart outlining several dimensions of these two animals. Have students discuss any similarities or differences.

2. A typical tepee required approximately twenty buffalo hides. Have students calculate the number of buffalo hides needed to house a village of fifty families; twenty-seven families; eighty-three families.

3. Invite students to create their own barter system similar to the one the Indians used. Ask students to bring in several items such as a blanket, a pair of shoes, a shirt, a toy gun, and the like. Ask students to establish a pricing guide that does not use money but rather is based on the estimated worth of those objects. Have students design a comparative shopping guide for the trading of common objects.

Music

1. An excellent recording to play for students is *Songs of Earth, Water, Fire, and Sky (Music of the American Indians)* New York: New World Records, 1976). After students have listened to several selections, ask them to interpret the meanings of those songs. Why did the Indians create songs about the forces of nature? What kinds of instruments were used to depict the forces of nature?

Social Studies

1. Divide the class into several groups. Have each group select and research a particular Indian tribe including their life styles, where they lived, some of their customs and traditions, whether they were farmers or hunters, types of dwellings, and so on. Each group should be prepared to collect their data into booklet form to be shared with other students in the class.

2. The National Geographic Society (Washington, DC) has an excellent filmstrip series entitled The Life of the American Indian (1977 [catalog no. 03243]). These two sound filmstrips provide valuable data on the Eastern, Plains, Northwestern, and Southwestern Indians of this country. A complementary video (also from the National Geographic Society) is *American Indians: A Brief History* (1985 [catalog no. 51004]).

Physical Education

1. Students may wish to play a modern version of the Indian game "Chunkey." In the game, a rimmed disk (a garbage can lid or small patio table top would make appropriate substitutes) is rolled down a grassy court. Two people run after the disk and throw wooden poles as close as possible to the spot where they expect the disk to fall over. The closest one wins!

Part 3
More Suggested Books for Reluctant Readers

The following lists collect many books recommended for reluctant readers. These lists are not intended to be definitive or exhaustive, but rather simply to offer you some books to consider for the reluctant readers in your classroom. You are encouraged to use these lists as starting points, supplementing them with your own favorites, the recommendations of colleagues, the reviews of literature in professional journals (see "Sources and Resources"), and, most important, the interests and suggestions of your students both current and past.

It is my hope that in these books you will discover a plethora of possibilities to incite, stimulate, and energize all the readers in your classroom. I hope your classroom will be filled with tales, novels, stories, fables, myths, legends, sagas, fantasies, and books of every genre. A classroom that overflows with literature is a classroom that promotes reading as a valuable and viable part of each and every student's life. Fill your classroom with books and you may fill the mind of even the most reluctant of readers with imagination, spirit, and endless opportunities for discovery and wonder.

■ ── ■

Amelia Bedelia by Peggy Parish. Harper & Row Junior Books, 1963.

Arthur's Baby by Marc Brown. Little, Brown, 1987.

Arthur's Funny Money by Lillian Hoban. Harper & Row Junior Books, 1981.

Babe the Gallant Pig by Dick King-Smith. Crown, 1983.

The Bears on Hemlock Mountain by Alice Dalgleish. Scribner, 1952.

The Best Christmas Pageant Ever by Barbara Robinson. Harper & Row Junior Books, 1972.

A Birthday Bike for Brimhall by Judy Delton. Carolrhoda, 1985.

Call for Mr. Sniff by Thomas P. Lewis. Harper & Row Junior Books, 1981.

Cam Jansen and the Mystery of the Stolen Corn Popper by David A. Adler. Viking Penguin, 1986.

The Case of the Cat's Meow by Crosby Bonsall. Harper & Row Junior Books, 1965.

The Cay by Theodore Taylor. Doubleday, 1969.

A Certain Small Sheperd by Rebecca Caudill. Henry Holt, 1965.

Chloe and Maude by Sandra Boynton. Little, Brown, 1983.

Clara and the Bookwagon by Nancy Levison. Harper, 1988.

Clyde Monster by Robert Crowe. Dutton, 1976.

Commander Toad and the Big Black Hole by Jane Yolen. Coward-McCann, 1983.

The Courage of Sarah Noble by Alice Dalgliesh. Scribner, 1954.

The Covered Bridge House and Other Poems by Kaye Starbird. Four Winds, 1979.

Daniel's Duck by Clyde Robert Bulla. Harper & Row Junior Books, 1979.

Dexter by Clyde Robert Bulla. Crowell, 1973.

A Dog Called Kitty by Bill Wallace. Holiday, 1980.

Don't Be Mad Ivy by Christine McConnell. Dial Books, 1981.

Dorrie and the Blue Witch by Patricia Coombs. Lothrop, 1964.

The Drinking Gourd by F. N. Monjo. Harper, 1970.

Four on the Shore by Edward Marshall. Dial Books, 1985.

Fox on Wheels by Edward Marshall. Dial Books, 1983.

Giant Kippernose and Other Stories by John Cunliffe. Deutsch, 1972.

Grasshopper and the Unwise Owl by Jim Slater. Holt, 1979.

Harry Kitten and Tucker Mouse by George Seldon. Farrar, 1986.

Helga's Dowry: A Troll Love Story by Tomie dePaola. Harcourt, 1977.

Help! I'm a Prisoner in the Library by Eth Clifford. Houghton Mifflin, 1979.

Henry and Ribsy by Beverly Cleary. Morrow, 1954.

Henry Huggins by Beverly Cleary. Morrow, 1950.

Henry Mudge and the Forever Sea by Cynthia Ryland. Bradbury Press, 1989.

The Hit Away Kid by Matt Christopher. Little, Brown, 1988.

Homer Price by Robert McClosky. Viking, 1943.

How My Parents Learned to Eat by Ina Friedman. Houghton Mifflin, 1984.

Hurricane by Faith McNulty. Harper, 1983.

Hurry Home, Candy by Meindert DeJong. Harper, 1953.

Ida Early Comes Over the Mountain by Robert Burch. Viking, 1980.

I'll Meet You at the Cucumbers by Lilian Moore. Atheneum, 1988.

In the Year of the Boar and Jackie Robinson by Bette Bao Lord. Harper, 1984.

The Indian in the Cupboard by Lynne Reid Banks. Doubleday, 1981.

Indian Summer by F. N. Monjo. Harper, 1968.

The Iron Giant by Ted Hughes. Harper, 1985.

The Island of the Skog by Steven Kellog. Dial Books, 1976.

Jacob Two-Two Meets the Hooded Fang by Mordecai Richler. Knopf, 1975.

Jenny Archer, Author by Ellen Conford. Little, Brown, 1989.

Just Plain Cat by Nancy Robinson. Four Winds, 1981.

Kick, Pass, and Run by Leonard Kessler. Harper, 1966.

King Bidgood's in the Bathtub by Audrey Wood. Harcourt, 1985.

Lafcadio, The Lion Who Shot Back by Shel Silverstein. Harper, 1963.

Leo and Emily's Big Ideas by Franz Brandenberg. Greenwillow, 1982.

Leprechauns Never Lie by Lorna Balian. Abingdon, 1980.

A Lion to Guard Us by Clyde Robert Bulla. Crowell, 1981.

Listen Children by Dorothy Strickland (ed.). Bantam Books, 1982.

The Littles by John Peterson. Scholastic, 1970.

The Lone Hunt by William O. Steele. Harcourt, 1976.

The Long Way Westward by Joan Sandin. Harper, 1989.

The Lucky Stone by Lucille Clifton. Delacorte, 1979.

M & M and the Haunted House Game by Pat Ross. Pantheon, 1980.

Magic Secrets by Rose Wyler and Gerald Ames. Harper, 1990.

The Maid of the North by Ethel Phelps. Holt, 1981.

McBroom Tells the Truth by Sid Fleischman. Little, Brown, 1966.

Misty of Chincoteague by Marguerite Henry. Rand McNally, 1947.

Mitzi and the Terrible Tyrannosaurus by Barbara Williams. Dutton, 1982.

Molly's Pilgrim by Barbara Cohen. Lothrop, 1983.

The Monster in the Third Dresser Drawer and Other Stories About Adam Joshua by Janet Smith. Harper, 1981.

The Monster's Ring by Bruce Coville. Pantheon, 1982.

Mouse and the Motorcycle by Beverly Cleary. Morrow, 1965.

Mr. Popper's Penguins by Richard Atwater and Florence Atwater. Little, Brown, 1938.

My Father's Dragon by Ruth S. Gannett. Random House, 1948.

My Twin Sister Erika by Ilse-Margaret Vogel. Harper, 1976.

Nana Upstairs and Nana Downstairs by Tomie dePaola. Putnam, 1973.

The Napping House by Audrey Wood. Harcourt, 1984.

Nate the Great Stalks Stupidweed by Marjorie Sharmot. Coward-McCann, 1986.

The Ordinary Princess by M. M. Kaye. Doubleday, 1984.

The Pain and the Great One by Judy Blume. Bradbury Press, 1974.

Pearl's Promise by Frank Asch. Delacorte, 1984.

Penrod's Pants by Mary Christian. Macmillan. 1986.

Porcupine's Pajama Party by Terry Harshman. Harper, 1988.

The Quilt Story by Tony Johnson. Putnam, 1985.

Ramona Forever by Beverly Cleary. Morrow, 1984.

Ramona the Pest by Beverly Cleary. Morrow, 1968.

The Random House Book of Poetry for Children by Jack Prelutsky (ed.). Random House, 1983.

Ready, Set, Robot! by Lillian Hoban and Phoebe Hoban. Harper, 1982.

The Secret Garden by Frances Hodgson Burnett. Lippincott, 1962.

See My Lovely Poison Ivy by Lilian Moore. Atheneum, 1975.

Selene Goes Home by Lucy Diggs. Atheneum, 1989.

The Sherluck Bones Mystery—Detective Book 1 by Jim Razzi and Mary Razzi. Bantam Books, 1981.

The Small Potatoes by Harriet Ziefert. Dell, 1984.

Star Mother's Youngest Child by Louise Moeri. Houghton Mifflin, 1975.

The Stories Julian Tells by Ann Cameron. Pantheon, 1981.

Super Duper Teddy by Johanna Hurwitz. Morrow, 1980.

Third Grade Is Terrible by Barbara Baker. Dutton, 1989.

Three up a Tree by James Marshall. Dial Books, 1986.

Thundercake by Patricia Polacco. Philomel, 1990.

Tut's Mummy by Judy Donnelly. Random House, 1988.

Us and Uncle Fraud by Lois Lowry. Houghton Mifflin, 1984.

Wagon Wheels by Barbara Brenner. Harper, 1978.

Warton and Morton by Russell Erikson. Morrow, 1976.

Watch Out! Man-eating Snake by Patricia Reilly Giff. Dell Publishing, 1988.

Watch the Stars Come Out by Rikki Levinson. Dutton, 1985.

When Bluebell Sang by Lisa Campbell Ernst. Bradbury Press, 1989.

Winnie-the-Pooh by A. A. Milne. Dutton, 1926.

The Witch of Fourth Street by Myron Levoy. Harper, 1972.

Zack's Alligator by Shirley Mozelle. Harper, 1989.

Zucchini by Barbara Dana. Harper, 1982.

Grades 4 and 5

The Accident by Carol Carrick. Seabury, 1976.

After the Rain by Norma Fox Mazer. Morrow, 1987.

Among the Dolls by William Sleator. Dutton, 1975.

Anastasia on Her Own by Lois Lowry. Houghton Mifflin, 1985.

And Nobody Knew They Were There by Otto Salassi. Greenwillow, 1984.

Angel's Mother's Wedding by Judy Delton. Houghton Mifflin, 1987.

The Bad Times of Irma Baumlein by Carol Brink. Macmillan, 1972.

The Bear's House by Marilyn Sachs. Doubleday, 1971.

The Black Stallion by Walter Farley. Random House, 1944.

The Borrowers Afloat by Mary Norton. Harcourt, 1959.

Bridge to Terabithia by Katherine Paterson. Crowell, 1977.

A Bundle of Sticks by Pat Rhoads Mauser. Atheneum, 1982.

Burnish Me Bright by Julia Cunningham. Dell Publishing, 1980.

Caddie Woodlawn by Carol Brink. Macmillan, 1935.

Call It Courage by Armstrong Sperry. Macmillan, 1940.

Captain Grey by Avi. Pantheon, 1977.

The Case of the Baker Street Irregulars by Robert Newman. Atheneum, 1978.

Catwings by Ursula LeGuin. Watts, 1988.

Charlotte's Web by E. B. White. Harper, 1952.

Chimps by Jane Goodall. Atheneum, 1989.

Cricket in Times Square by George Seldon. Farrar, 1960.

Danny the Champion of the World by Roald Dahl. Knopf, 1978.

Dicey's Song by Cynthia Voigt. Atheneum, 1982.

Dollhouse Murders by Betty Wright. Holiday, 1983.

Emily Upham's Revenge by Avi. Pantheon, 1978.

The Enormous Egg by Oliver Butterworth. Little, Brown, 1956.

Family Secrets: Five Very Important Stories by Susan Shreve. Knopf, 1979.

Freckle Juice by Judy Blume. Four Winds, 1971.

From the Mixed-up Files of Mrs. Basil E. Frankweiler by E. L. Konigsburg. Atheneum, 1967.

Gentle Ben by Walt Morey. Dutton, 1965.

Grandma Didn't Wave Back by Rose Blue. Watts, 1972.

Grey Cloud by Charlotte Graeber. Four Winds, 1979.

Herbie Jones and the Monster Ball by Suzy Kline. Putnam, 1988.

Hey, What's Wrong with This One? by Maia Wojciechowska. Harper, 1969.

Humbug Mountain by Sid Fleischman. Little, Brown, 1978.

The Hundred Dresses by Eleanor Estes. Harcourt, 1944.

If I Were in Charge of the World and Other Worries by Judith Viorst. Atheneum, 1981.

Inside My Feet: The Story of a Giant by Richard Kennedy. Harper, 1979.

Into the Painted Bear Lair by Pamela Stearns. Houghton Mifflin, 1976.

Introducing Shirley Braverman by Hilma Wolitzer. Farrar, 1975.

Island of the Blue Dolphins by Scott O'Dell. Houghton Mifflin, 1960.

It Ain't All for Nothin' by Walter Dean Myers. Viking, 1978.

It's a Mile from Here to Glory by Robert C. Lee. Little, Brown, 1972.

J. T. by Jane Wagner. Dell, 1971.

James and the Giant Peach by Roald Dahl. Knopf, 1961.

The Lion, the Witch and the Wardrobe by C. S. Lewis. Macmillan, 1950.

Little House in the Big Woods by Laura Ingalls Wilder. Harper, 1932.

Long Journey by Barbara Corcoran. Atheneum, 1970.

Mandy by Julie Edwards. Harper, 1971.

Me and Caleb by Franklyn Mayer. Scholastic, 1982.

The Midnight Fox by Betsy Byars. Viking, 1968.

Mine for Keeps by Jean Little. Little, Brown, 1962.

Mishmash and the Big Fat Problem by Molly Cone. Archway, 1982.

Mrs. Fish, Ape, and Me, the Dump Queen by Norma Fox Mazer. Dutton, 1980.

Mrs. Frisby and the Rats of NIMH by Robert C. O'Brien. Atheneum, 1971.

My Brother Sam Is Dead by James Collier and Christopher Collier. Scholastic, 1977.

My Dad Lives in a Downtown Hotel by Peggy Mann. Doubleday, 1973.

My Side of the Mountain by Jean George. Dutton, 1959.

The Night of the Twisters by Ivy Ruckman. Harper, 1984.

Nightmares: Poems to Trouble Your Sleep by Jack Prelutsky. Greenwillow, 1976.

No Beasts! No Children! by Beverly Keller. Lothrop, 1983.

No One Is Going to Nashville by Mavis Jukes. Knopf, 1983.

North to Freedom by Anne Holm. Harcourt, 1974.

Orp by Suzy Kline. Putnam, 1989.

Our John Willie by Catherine Cookson. Bobbs-Merrill, 1974.

Peppermints in the Parlor by Barbara Wallace. Atheneum, 1980.

Pinch by Larry Callen. Little, Brown, 1976.

Pippi Longstocking by Astrid Lindgren. Viking, 1950.

Prisoners at the Kitchen Table by Barbara Holland. Clarion, 1979.

R, My Name Is Rosie by Barbara Cohen. Lothrop, 1978.

Rain of Fire by Marion Bauer. Clarion, 1983.

The Real Thief by William Steig. Farrar, 1973.

Remembering the Good Times by Richard Peck. Delacorte, 1985.

Rosy Cole's Great American Guilt Club by Sheila Greenwald. Atlantic Monthly, 1985.

Sara Crewe by Frances Burnett. Putnam, 1981.

The Search for Delicious by Natalie Babbitt. Farrar, 1969.

The Secret of the Seal by Deborah Davis. Crown, 1989.

The Shadow Nose by Elizabeth Levy. Morrow, 1983.

Shadow of a Bull by Maia Wojciechowska. Atheneum, 1964.

The Show-and-Tell War by Janice Lee Smith. Harper, 1988.

The Sign of the Beaver by Elizabeth Speare. Houghton Mifflin, 1983.

Sing Down the Moon by Scott O'Dell. Houghton Mifflin, 1970.

The Snailman by Brenda Sivers. Little, Brown, 1978.

Snow Treasure by Marie McSwigan. Dutton, 1942.

Soup by Robert Newton Peck. Knopf, 1974.

Stone Fox by John Gardiner. Crowell, 1980.

Storm Boy by Colin Thiele, Harper, 1978.

Storms by Seymour Simon. Morrow, 1989.

A Stranger Came Ashore by Mollie Hunter. Harper, 1975.

The Summer of the Swans by Betsy Byars. Viking, 1970.

Tales of a Fourth Grade Nothing by Judy Blume. Dutton, 1972.

A Taste of Blackberries by Doris Smith. Crowell, 1973.

Tomboy by Norma Klein. Four Winds, 1978.

The Trading Game by Alfred Slote. Lippincott, 1990.

Trouble River by Betsy Byars. Viking, 1969.

Tuck Everlasting by Natalie Babbitt. Farrar, 1975.

Twenty and Ten by Claire Bishop. Viking, 1952.

The Velveteen Rabbit by Margery Williams. Knopf, 1985.

Weird Henry Berg by Sarah Sargent. Crown, 1980.

The Westing Game by Ellen Raskin. Dutton, 1978.

What Happened in Hamelin by Gloria Skurzynski. Four Winds, 1979.

Where the Lilies Bloom by Vera Cleaver and Bill Cleaver. Lippincott, 1969.

Where the Red Fern Grows by Wilson Rawls. Doubleday, 1961.

Where the Sidewalk Ends by Shel Silverstein. Harper, 1974.

Wild Violets by Phyllis Green. Dell Publishing, 1980.

The Wish Giver by Bill Brittain. Harper, 1983.

The Wolves of Willoughby Chase by Joan Aiken. Doubleday, 1962.

The Wonderful Story of Henry Sugar and Six More by Roald Dahl. Knopf, 1977.

RESOURCE BIBLIOGRAPHY

Sources for Children's Literature

Arbuthnot, May Hill. *Children's Books Too Good to Miss.* 8th ed. Cleveland, OH: Press of Case Western Reserve University, 1989.

Barstow, Barbara. *Beyond Picture Books: A Guide to First Readers.* New York: R. R. Bowker, 1989.

Children's Books: Awards and Prizes. New York: Children's Book Council, 1981.

The Children's Catalog. New York: H. W. Wilson Co.

Children's Choices. Newark, DE: International Reading Association (issued each year).
A compilation of the best books published each year as selected by teachers and librarians.

Cranciolo, Patricia. *Picture Books for Children.* Chicago: American Library Association, 1990.

Dreyer, Sharon. *The Bookfinder: When Kids Need Books.* Circle Pines, MN: American Guidance Service, 1985.

Eakin, Mary. *Subject Index to Books for Primary Grades.* 3d ed. Chicago: American Library Association, 1967.

The Elementary School Library Collection. 15th ed. Williamsport, PA: Brodart, 1986.

Ettlinger, John. *Choosing Books for Young People, Volume 2: A Guide to Criticism and Bibliography, 1976-1984.* Phoenix, AZ: Oryx, 1987.

Gillespie, John. *Best Books for Children: Preschool through Grade Six.* 4th ed. New York: Bowker, 1990.
A listing of over 500 subject headings and 11,000 books arranged alphabetically.

Gillespie, John. *Elementary School Paperback Collection.* Chicago: American Library Association, 1985.

Hearne, Betsy. *Choosing Books for Children.* New York: Delacorte, 1990.

Jett-Simpson, Mary. *Adventuring with Books: A Booklist for Pre-K — Grade 6.* Urbana, IL: National Council of Teachers of English, 1989.

Kimmel, Margaret M., and Elizabeth Segel. *For Reading Out Loud!* New York: Delacorte, 1988.
Guidelines to help teachers and parents select books appropriate to the ages and interests of all youngsters.

Kobrin, Beverly. *Eyeopeners! How to Choose and Use Children's Books About Real People, Places, and Things.* New York: Viking, 1988.
A thorough, annotated bibliography of nonfiction books. Includes a variety of books on various topics along with a potpourri of extending activities and projects for selected books.

Lima, Carol, and John A. Lima. *A to Zoo: Subject Access to Children's Picture Books.* 3d ed. New York: R. R. Bowker, 1989.
An all-inclusive listing of more than twelve thousand titles catalogued under seven hundred subjects. This is *the* comprehensive collection of picture book titles.

Lukens, Rebecca. *A Critical Handbook of Children's Literature*. Glenview, IL: Scott, Foresman, 1986.

Lynn, Ruth N. *Fantasy for Children: An Annotated Checklist and Reference Guide*. 2d ed. New York: R. R. Bowker, 1983.
An extensive listing of more than two thousand recommended titles.

Monson, Dianne. *Adverturing with Books: A Booklist for Pre-K — Grade 6*. Urbana, IL: National Council of Teachers of English, 1985.
An annotated bibliography of over seventeen hundred books appropriate for classroom and home use.

The New York Times Parent's Guide to the Best Books for Children. New York: Times Books, 1988.

Norton, Donna E. *Through the Eyes of a Child: An Introduction to Children's Literature*. New York: Merrill, 1991.
A marvelous introduction to children's literature, the different genres, and ways to use it productively in the classroom. Contains hundreds of annotated listings.

Pilla, Marianne L. *The Best: High/Low Books for Reluctant Readers*. Englewood, CO: Libraries Unlimited, 1990.
A carefully researched bibliography of high-interest, low-vocabulary books for students in third through twelfth grades. Includes books from many subject areas.

Rollock, Barbara. *The Black Experience in Children's Books*. New York: The New York Public Library, 1984.
Books on black life in America, Europe, Africa, and the Caribbean are covered in this annotated bibliography.

Schon, Isabel. *A Hispanic Heritage: A Guide to Juvenile Books About Hispanic Peoples and Cultures*. Metuchen, NJ: Scarecrow Press, 1980.
Offers extensive reviews of books dealing with Hispanic cultures around the world.

Taylor, Barbara M., and Dianne L. Monson. *Reading Together: Helping Children Get a Good Start in Reading*. Glenview, IL: Scott, Foresman, 1991.
A rich and wonderful book full of activities and strategies to promote reading at home and at school. The second half of the book has an extensive annotated bibliography of books recommended for children at different levels of reading ability and grade levels.

Trelease, Jim. *The Read Aloud Handbook*. New York: Penguin Books, 1985.
Wonderful ideas and suggestions for making reading a natural and normal part of children's lives. Includes an extensive listing of quality literature in all subject areas.

Vandergrift, Kay. *Child and Story: The Literary Connection*. Neal-Schuman, 1980.

Teacher Resource Books

Barchers, Suzanne. *Creating and Managing the Literate Classroom*. Englewood, CO: Libraries Unlimited, 1990.
A creative and insightful guide on the how-to's of establishing a literature-based curriculum.

Fredericks, Anthony D. *Social Studies through Children's Literature*. Englewood, CO: Libraries Unlimited, 1991.
A complete guide on the effective implementation of literature into the social studies curriculum. Contains many lists and resources for teachers.

Garrity, Linda. *After the Story's Over*. Glenview, IL: Scott, Foresman, 1991.
A collection of pre-reading and post-reading activities and projects for eighty-eight popular children's books.

Garrity, Linda. *The Gingerbread Guide*. Glenview, IL: Scott, Foresman, 1987.
This book contains a variety of ideas and strategies to incorporate popular folktales into the curriculum.

Hancock, Joelie, and Susan Hill, eds. *Literature-Based Reading Programs at Work.* Portsmouth, NH: Heinemann, 1987.
A collection of twelve articles by Australian and New Zealand teachers on making the change from a basal-based reading program to one that is literature-based.

Raines, Shirley, and Robert Canady. *More Story S-T-R-E-T-C-H-E-R-S: More Activities to Expand Children's Favorite Books.* Mt. Ranier, MD: Gryphon House, 1991.
Ninety books, mostly at the primary level, and a variety of extending activities highlight this informative book.

Rothlein, Liz, and Anita M. Meinbach. *The Literature Connection.* Glenview, IL: Scott, Foresman, 1991.
A complete guide to the implementation and maintenance of a literature-based curriculum.

Whole Language Resource Books

Barrs, M. *Primary Language Record.* Portsmouth, NH: Heinemann, 1990.

Butler, Andrea, and Jan Turbill. *Towards a Reading-Writing Classroom.* Portsmouth, NH: Heinemann, 1984.

Calkins, Lucy. *The Art of Teaching Writing.* Portsmouth, NH: Heinemann, 1986.

Cambourne, Brian. *The Whole Story.* New York: Scholastic, 1988.

Eggleton, J. *Whole Language Evaluation: Reading, Writing, and Speaking.* San Diego, CA: Wright, 1990.

Goodman, Ken. *What's Whole in Whole Languages.* Portsmouth, NH: Heinemann, 1986.

Goodman, Ken, Yetta Goodman, and W. Hood. *Whole Language Evaluation Book.* Portsmouth, NH: Heinemann, 1989.

Graves, Donald. *Build a Literate Classroom.* Portsmouth, NH: Heinemann, 1990.

Holdaway, Don. *The Foundations of Literacy.* Portsmouth, NH: Heinemann, 1979.

Mooney, M. *Reading to, with, and by Children.* Katonah, NY: Richard Owen, 1990.

Pappas, C., B. Keifer, and L. Levstik. *An Integrated Language Perspective in the Elementary School: Theory into Action.* New York: Longman, 1990.

Routman, Reggie. *Transitions: From Literature to Literacy.* Portsmouth, NH: Heinemann, 1988.

Strickland, Dorothy, and Leslie Morrow. *Emerging Literacy: Young Children Learn to Read and Write.* Newark, DE: International Reading Association, 1989.

Weaver, Constance. *Understanding Whole Language: From Principles to Practice.* Portsmouth, NH: Heinemann, 1990.

Review Sources

The ALAN Review. National Council of Teachers of English, 1111 Kenyon Road, Urbana, IL 61801.

Bookbird. International Periodical on Literature for Children and Young Adults, Publishing Firm ARNIS, Bergensvej 5, DK-6230 Roderko, Denmark.

Booklist. American Library Association, 50 East Huron Street, Chicago, IL 60611.

Booklures, Inc. P.O. Box 9450, O'Fallon, MO 63366.

Book Review Digest. Wilson, New York, NY.

The Bulletin of the Center for Children's Books. Graduate Library School, University of Chicago, Chicago, IL 60637.

Children's Literature Association Quarterly. Children's Literature Association, Purdue University Press, West Lafayette, IN 47907.

The Five Owls. 2004 Sheridan Avenue South, Minneapolis, MN 55405.
  A wonderful publication of book reviews and fascinating articles about the many dimensions of children's literature. A must for any school library or reading center.

The Horn Book. Horn Book Inc., 14 Beacon Street, Boston, MA 02108.

Instructor. Scholastic, Inc., P.O. Box 2039, Mahopac, NJ 10541.

The Kobrin Letter: Concerning Children's Books about Real People, Places and Things. 732 Greer Road, Palo Alto, CA 94303.
  Insightful reviews of nonfiction books for readers at all grade levels, interests, and abilities. The pre-eminent review guide of nonfiction.

Language Arts. National Council of Teachers of English, 1111 Kenyon Road, Urbana, IL 61801.

Learning. P.O. Box 51593, Boulder, CO 80321-1593.

The Lion and the Unicorn. Journals Publishing Division, The Johns Hopkins University Press, 701 West 40th Street, Suite 275, Baltimore, MD 21211.

The New Advocate. P.O. Box 809, Needham Heights, MA 02194.

The Reading Teacher. International Reading Association, Newark, DE 19714.
  The October issue for each year includes "Children's Choices," an extensive review of the best in children's literature from the past year.

School Library Journal (Star Track). P.O. Box 1978, Marion, OH 43306.

Teacher. P.O. Box 2091, Marion, OH 43305-2091.

Teaching K-8. P.O. Box 54808, Boulder, CO 80322-4808.
  Carol Hurst's column and her frequent articles are a must for those seeking to promote literature connections in the classroom or reading center.

Top of the News. American Library Association, 50 E. Huron Street, Chicago, IL 60611.

VOYA: Voice of Youth Advocates. Scarecrow Press, Department VOYA, 52 Liberty Street, P.O. Box 4167, Metuchen, NJ 09884.

The Web. Center for Language, Literature, and Reading, Ohio State University, Columbus, OH 43210.

Book Clubs for Students

Scholastic Book Clubs. 2931 East McCarty Street, P.O. Box 7500, Jefferson City, MO 65102.

Troll Book Clubs. 320 Route 17, Mahwah, NJ 07498.

The Trumpet Club. P.O. Box 604, Holmes, PA 19092.

Weekly Reader Paperback Clubs. 4343 Equity Drive, P.O. Box 16628, Columbus, OH 43272.

A Potpourri of Possibilities

Authors of Books for Young People—2nd Edition. Edited by Martha Ward and Dorothy Marquant. Metuchen, NJ: Scarecrow Press, 1971.
Complete biographical information on many of the world's most popular children's authors is offered in this volume. This is a valuable addition to discussions about selected authors. A supplement to the second edition was published in 1979.

Children's Book Council. 67 Irving Place, New York, NY 10003.
Write for a current list of children's book publishers that includes names, addresses, and telephone numbers. The CBC also features newsletter interviews, articles, and giveaway items.

Consumer Information Center. Pueblo, CO 81009.
Write for a copy of this all-purpose catalog listing over two hundred federal publications, many of which are free.

The Council on Interracial Books for Children. 1841 Broadway, New York, NY 10023.
This organization has a variety of pamphlets on selecting sexually and racially unbiased books for children.

I Can Be a.... Children's Press, Chicago.
This is a series of children's books about different occupations. Included are books about computer operators, doctors, fire fighters, teachers, musicians, television camera operators, and truck drivers.

New True Books. Children's Press, Chicago.
This series of children's books offers varied and informative insights into a host of topics. Descriptive photographs highlight each book.

Society for Visual Education. 1345 Diversey Parkway, Chicago, IL 60614.
Write for information on the films and videos in their Black Heroes series.

Book Wholesalers

Baker and Taylor. 652 East Main Street, P.O. Box 6920, Bridgewater, NJ 08807.

Book Wholesalers, Inc. 2025 Leestown Road, Lexington, KY 40511.

Bound to Stay Bound. West Morton Road, Jacksonville, IL 62560.

Brodart. 500 Arch Street, Williamsport, PA 17705.

INDEX

About the Author

Anthony D. Fredericks

Anthony D. Fredericks received his bachelor of arts degree in history from the University of Arizona, his master's degree in reading from Kutztown State College in Pennsylvania, and his doctor of education degree in reading from Lehigh University.

Tony has been a classroom teacher and reading specialist in public and private schools for more than fifteen years. He is a frequent presenter and storyteller at conferences, reading councils, schools, and inservice meetings throughout the United States and Canada. The author or coauthor of more than two hundred articles and fifteen books, he has written for *The Reading Teacher, Reading Today,* and *Teaching K-8.* He is recipient of many education awards, including the Innovative Teaching Award from the Pennsylvania State Education Association.

Tony currently resides in Glen Rock, Pennsylvania, with his wife, Phyllis, two children, Rebecca and Jonathan, and four cats. He is an Assistant Professor of Education at York College, York, Pennsylvania, where he teaches methods courses in reading, language arts, science, and social studies.